D0899598

The University of Chicago School Mathematics Project

Advanced Algebra

Computer Masters

BASIC programming and computer graphing activities

30 reproducible blackline masters with BASIC
programming and computer graphing activities
correlated to individual lessons in UCSMP
Advanced Algebra

Scott, Foresman and Company
Editorial Offices: Glenview, Illinois Regional Offices:
Sunnyvale, California • Tucker, Georgia • Glenview,
Illinois • Oakland, New Jersey • Dallas, Texas

ISBN: 0-673-45345-6

5678910-PAT-94939291

Contents

About the Computer Masters

The Computer Masters in this book provide problems for students to solve using either: (1) short BASIC programs, provided on the Master itself, which students type into the computer, or (2) a computer graphing program. (**Computer Master 27** involves both BASIC and graphing.) Computer graphing programs are commonly called "function plotters," "function graphers," "plotters," "equations graphers," or, simply, "graphers." The term *grapher* is used throughout the Computer Masters involving graphing activities and refers to any such computer graphing software. Graphing software for the Apple® II and IBM® PC/PS/2® series is available from Scott, Foresman in the Scott, Foresman *Algebra/Advanced Algebra* Software package.

The Computer Masters provided in this book are reproducible. It is intended that a copy of each master be made for each student in your class. The activities can be completed individually by students working alone, each at his or her own computer, or in small groups or as a whole-class activity.

BASIC Programs

Eleven of the Computer Masters for *Advanced Algebra* involve entering into the computer a BASIC program that is provided on the worksheet and analyzing the program in terms of its mathematics. In this way, the BASIC programs provide representations and uses of the mathematics taught in the *Advanced Algebra* lesson to which the worksheet is correlated. No Computer Master requires students to compose a BASIC program from scratch.

Computer Masters involving a BASIC program usually contain one or more items asking the student to modify one or more lines in the program to achieve a desired change in the program's output. Such problems require an understanding of the mathematics in the appropriate lesson of *Advanced Algebra,* and not an in-depth understanding of programming of BASIC. Any information about BASIC or about programming that the student needs to know in order to complete an activity is provided on the Computer Master worksheet itself.

The Computer Masters assume the use of AppleSoft® BASIC. Minor modifications may be necessary in some instances for the programs to run correctly on IBM PCs and PS/2s. Any difficulties should be easily remedied by referring to your IBM BASIC manual.

Graphing Activities

Twenty of the Computer Masters provide computer graphing activities. These can be completed as is or with minor modifications using most available graphing software for the Apple or IBM.

Common variations among graphers are described below. This discussion may help you adapt the graphing activities in the Computer Masters for use with your grapher.

Graphers: Notation

Some graphers use function notation (e.g., $f(x) = 2x$). Others use equation form (e.g., $y = 2x$). If you have a grapher that uses function notation and your students are not familiar with that notation, explain to them that the $f(x)$ for any x will be the same as the y value for that x. *Note:* **Computer Masters 12, 13, 16, 24,** and **26** use function notation.

Most graphers require that you enter equations or expressions using BASIC notation (e.g., $y = 2 * x \wedge 2$). This notably involves using the symbols * for multiplication, $\wedge$ for exponentiation, and / for division. Some graphers allow you to represent multiplication as you would see it in a book: $2x$, without the * symbol.

The documentation for most graphers includes a list of mathematical functions they support, with instructions for entering those functions.

Graphers: Identifying Specific Coordinates on a Graph

Some graphers offer a cursor that can be moved anywhere on the graphing screen or along a graph. For any selected position of the cursor, the program displays the coordinates of that point. From program to program, the cursor can be placed to varying degrees of accuracy. If your grapher offers a movable cursor, experiment to discover how accurately you can place a cursor on a graph.

If your grapher does not allow you to display the coordinates of any point on a graph by moving a cursor to that point, it probably does allow the option to rescale the graph in such a way that you can read from the graph a reasonably accurate estimate of a y-value for any x-value. Your grapher may also allow you to display a table of x and y values along any x-interval. From this table, it may be possible to read the y-value for any x-value, assuming the interval chosen is appropriate.

In these Computer Masters, whenever students are asked to estimate the y-value for a given x, they are directed to do so by rescaling. (Some graphers refer to rescaling as "zooming.") Whenever the student is directed to rescale to find a value, the student can find that value using the movable cursor if it is available.

Graphers: Intervals

It is probably safe to say that all graphers allow you to set the x and y intervals on which to graph a function or equation. However, different graphers handle differently the process of defining intervals and the manner in which the intervals for the current graph are indicated on the screen. Some graphers have you define the x interval (domain) on which to graph immediately after you have entered the equation or function. Many graphers automatically calculate the y interval. Other graphers use default x and y intervals until you specifically indicate that you want to change those intervals. The changing of intervals is often offered as a menu choice.

Graphers: Inverses

Some, but not all, graphers offer automatic graphing of inverses of functions. If your grapher does not offer the option to graph automatically the inverse of a function, then to complete **Computer Master 16** your students will have to begin each problem by writing the inverse of the given function. Then they will enter the inverse of the given function as a function.

Graphers: Exponentials

Some graphers do not accept an equation of the form $y = a^x$ for any value of a given by the student. **Computer Masters 19, 21,** and **22** can only be completed using a grapher that allows graphing of an equation in this form.

Graphers: Conics

Not all graphers have the capability of accepting conic equations. Students will not be able to complete **Computer Master 28** unless your grapher can accept and graph conic equations.

Graphers: Inequalities

Most graphing software does not offer the option of graphing inequalities. To complete **Computer Master 5,** students should graph the equation that corresponds to each inequality given on the Master and use that graph to determine the solution to the corresponding problem.

Graphers: Compositions of Functions

In **Computer Master 13,** students explore compositions of functions. Many, but not all, graphers allow students the capability of defining a function in terms of another function. If your grapher does not offer the option to build functions in this way, and if you wish to have your students complete **Computer Master 13,** you may have students write the composite function and then graph that function as an alternative to having the students define $f(x)$ and $g(x)$ and then graph $f(g(x))$.

Correlation of *Advanced Algebra* Computer Masters to Textbook Lessons

Lesson	Computer Master	Software to Be Used with Computer Master
1-3; 1-4	1	BASIC
2-7	2	grapher
3-2	3	grapher
3-6; 3-7	4	BASIC
3-8	5	grapher
4-8	6	grapher
5-2	7	grapher
5-8	8	grapher
6-2	9	grapher
6-4	10	grapher
6-7	11	grapher
7-1	12	BASIC
7-3	13	grapher
7-4	14	BASIC
7-5	15	grapher
7-6; 7-7	16	grapher
8-2	17	BASIC
8-3	18	BASIC
9-1; 9-2	19	grapher
9-4	20	BASIC
9-5	21	grapher
9-9	22	grapher
10-3	23	BASIC
10-9	24	grapher
10-10	25	BASIC
11-4	26	grapher
11-5	27	grapher, BASIC
12-8	28	grapher
12-9; 12-10	29	grapher
13-1; 13-2; 13-4	30	BASIC

Computer Master 1
Using BASIC with Sequences

Computer languages use commands, functions and arithmetic symbols. In BASIC most of these have the same meaning as in everyday use. However several important exceptions or abbreviations are: * for multiplication, / for division, ∧ for powers, and SQR for square root.

1. The following BASIC program can be used to produce number sequences:

```
10   FOR N = 1 to 6
20     LET T = 5 + 4 * (N − 1)
30     PRINT T
40   NEXT N
50   END
```

  a. RUN the program. Write the sequence that is produced. _____

  b. Examine line 20 of the program. Is the formula explicit or recursive? _____

  c. Explain how to modify the program so it prints 20 terms of the same sequence. RUN the program to check that it works.

---

2. Rewrite the expression $\dfrac{3(N − 1)}{2}$ in BASIC.

Then change line 20 in the program above to include the expression. RUN the program to print a sequence generated by the expression. _____

3. Change the program to generate powers of two. Use it to compute 2^{12}. _____

4. Another BASIC program to produce sequences is as follows:

```
10   LET T = 5
20   FOR N = 1 TO 10
30     PRINT T
40     LET T = T + 4
50   NEXT N
60   END
```

  a. Is the formula in line 40 explicit or recursive? _____

  b. RUN the program. Write the sequence that is produced. _____

Computer Master 1   (page 2)

c. Modify the program to print a sequence in which the first term is 86 and each term exceeds the succeeding term by eleven.   _____

d. Modify the program to print a sequence in which the first term is 9 and each term is five times the preceding term.   _____

5. Each term T in the Fibonacci sequence is the sum of the two preceding terms R and S. Complete the program below to print the Fibonacci sequence:

```
 10   LET R = ___
 20   PRINT R
 30   LET S = ___
 40   PRINT S
 50   FOR N = 3 TO 10
 60     LET T = ___
 70     PRINT T
 80     LET R = ___
 90     LET S = ___
100   NEXT N
110   END
```

a. RUN the program and copy or print out the output.   _____

b. Modify the program so it prints the first 22 terms of the Fibonacci sequence.   _____

c. Change line 70 to

```
70   PRINT R; : HTAB 10: PRINT S; : HTAB 20; PRINT T;
         : HTAB 30: PRINT S/R
```

Describe the pattern in the column giving the ratio of S to R.

_____

Computer Master 2

Graphing Variation

A computer grapher can be used to draw graphs of formulas representing direct and inverse variation. Use a computer grapher to do each of the following problems.

1. On the same pair of axes, graph the two equations given below. For each equation, identify whether the variation is direct or inverse.

   a. $y = \dfrac{x}{4}$ Variation: _____

   b. $y = \dfrac{4}{x}$ Variation: _____

   c. Describe the difference between the two graphs.

   _____

2. a. On one set of axes graph $y = 3x^2$ and $y = -3x^2$.

   b. On the same set of axes graph another pair of equations that are reflection images of each other. Record the four equations below.

   _____   _____   _____   _____

   c. For each equation, identify whether the variation is direct or inverse.

   _____   _____   _____   _____

3. On the same, new pair of axes, graph $y = \dfrac{1}{x}$ and $y = \dfrac{1}{x^2}$.

   a. How are the graphs similar?

   _____

   b. How are the graphs different?

   _____

   c. Rescale to examine the graphs on the window $0 < x < 2, 0 < y < 1$.
      For what positive values of x is $\dfrac{1}{x^2} > \dfrac{1}{x}$?   _____

   d. For what positive values of x is $\dfrac{1}{x} > \dfrac{1}{x^2}$?   _____

Computer Master 2 (page 2)

4. a. Make a hypothesis as to what the graph of $y = \dfrac{1}{x^3}$ should look like. Describe how you expect its graph to be similar to and different from the graphs for the two equations given in problem 3, above.

_____

_____

b. Test your hypothesis by graphing the equation.

5. a. For any equation $y = \dfrac{k}{x}$ or $y = \dfrac{k}{x^2}$, what happens to the graph as the value of k increases?

_____

b. Make a conjecture about the effect of k on the graph of $y = \dfrac{k}{x^3}$. Test your conjecture by graphing. Summarize your results.

_____

_____

In 6-9, graph the equation on the interval $-5 < x < 5$, each on a different pair of axes. For each graph, give an equation for all asymptotes and axes of symmetry, if any.

6. $y = \dfrac{1}{x^2} - 1$ asymptotes: _____

           axes of symmetry: _____

7. $y = \dfrac{1}{(x - 1)^2}$ asymptotes: _____

           axes of symmetry: _____

8. $y = \dfrac{4}{(x + 2)^2}$ asymptotes: _____

           axes of symmetry: _____

9. $y = \dfrac{4}{x^2} + 2$ asymptotes: _____

           axes of symmetry: _____

Computer Master 2 (for use with Lesson 2-7)
Advanced Algebra © Scott, Foresman and Co.

Computer Master 3

Graphing $y = mx + b$

Use a separate pair of axes for each problem.

1. Graph $y = 2x + 7$ (Use $f(x) = 2x + 7$). On the same axes, graph $y = 2x - 4$ and $y = 2x$. Describe in words the relationship among the three lines. Graph a fourth line $y = 2x + 3$. How is this line related to the other lines?

   _____

2. Graph $y = x - 1$, $y = 2x - 1$, and $y = -5x - 1$. Describe in words the relationship among the three lines. Describe what you think the graph of $y = -1 - x$ will look like. Graph the fourth line to test your conclusion.

   _____

3. Graph $y = 2x$, $y = 4x$, and $y = 8x$. Describe in words any pattern that can be observed. Graph $y = \frac{1}{2}x$, $y = \frac{1}{4}x$, and $y = \frac{1}{8}x$. Is there a similarity between the relationships among the two sets of lines?

   _____

4. Graph the lines defined by the equations, $y = 4x + 2$, $y = 8 - x$, and $y = -x - 4$. Graph a fourth line that has -5 as its y-intercept and completes a parallelogram. What is an equation of the line?

   _____

For problems 5–6, use the graph to estimate the value. Then use the Trace option or the Points and Lines option to find the exact value. Use the rescaling option as needed.

5. Graph $y = 5x - 3$.

   a. Find y when $x = 2$ _____

   b. Find y when $x = -2$ _____

   c. Find x when $y = 7$ _____

   d. Find y when $x = 2.6$ _____

   e. Find x when $y = 9$ _____

Computer Master 3 (page 2)

6. Temperature measurements can be converted from a Celsius scale to a Fahrenheit equivalent using the formula $F = 1.8C + 32$. Rescale so that the lower and upper limits for both the x-axis and the y-axis are -100 and 100 respectively. Graph the formula to find:

a. the Fahrenheit equivalent of 15°C.   _____

b. the Celsius equivalent of 23°F.   _____

c. the Celsius equivalent of 71.6°F.   _____

d. the Fahrenheit equivalent of -12°C.   _____

Computer Master 3 (for use with Lesson 3-2)
Advanced Algebra © Scott, Foresman and Co.

Computer Master 4
Using BASIC with Arithmetic Sequences

In a previous activity BASIC programs were developed to produce number sequences with either explicit or recursive formulas.

1. Consider the program below. The IF . . THEN statement in line 40 is used to terminate a run of the program after a specified number of terms.

```
10   LET N = 1
20   LET T = 5 − 4 * (N − 1)
30   PRINT N, T
40   IF N = 10 THEN 70
50   LET N = N + 1
60   GOTO 20
70   END
```

   a. RUN the program. How many lines are printed? What is the last line printed?   _____

   b. How should line 40 be revised so the program will print exactly 15 terms of the sequence 5, 1, −3, −7, . . . ?   _____

   Check your answer by running the program with a revision of line 40.

In 2–4, revise lines 20 and 40 so that the program can produce each of the following arithmetic sequences. Attach a copy of your program and the output.

2. The first fifteen terms of 7, 16, 25, 34, 43, . . .

_____

3. The first 20 terms of 4, −8, −20, −32, −44, . . .

_____

4. The first 12 terms of a sequence in which the first term is −33 and each term exceeds the preceeding term by 5.

_____

5. A formula for the sum of the measures of the interior angles of any polygon is $S = 180(N − 2)$ where N is the number of sides in the polygon.

   a. Revise the program to print a table with N and S for the first ten polygons starting with a triangle. Record the lines you changed.

_____

   b. According to your table, if the sum of the measures of the angles of a polygon is 1440, how many sides does the polygon have?   _____

Computer Master 4   (page 2)

6. It may be useful to stop a program when any term reaches or exceeds a certain value. For instance, if line 40 is changed as follows

$$40 \quad \text{IF } T <= -51 \text{ THEN } 70$$

then the program will print N and T as long as $T > -51$. But as soon as $T \le -51$ the program will stop. Revise lines 20, 30, and 40 so that the program prints a table with the sequence 19, 31, 43, 55, . . . and then stops once any term is greater than or equal to 200.

---

7. Public television station Channel 58 has a goal of raising \$58,585.85 in its subscription pledge drive on January 31 from 9 am to 9 pm. A subscription costs \$58.58. By 8:30 pm \$56,998.34 has been pledged and the anxious station manager decides to create additional incentive by starting a countdown of the number of pledges still needed.
Use the BASIC program to determine that
number.   _____

8. Revise the program to use a recursive formula. Use the program to print a table with the first ten terms of the sequence 16, 7, -2, -11, -20, . . .

---

9. The following program uses recursive formulas with two variables to create a sequence:

```
10   LET T = 5
20   LET R = 2
30   FOR N = 1 TO 10
40     PRINT N, T
50     LET T = T + R
60     LET R = R + 2
70   NEXT N
80   END
```

a. RUN the program. Is the sequence arithmetic? Why or why not?

---

b. Change line 40 to print the values of N, T, and R, then RUN it again. Describe in words the sequence that is arithmetic.

---

c. Change the initial values of T and R and use the program to produce a sequence of square numbers.

Computer Master 4 (for use with Lessons 3-6 and 3-7)
Advanced Algebra © Scott, Foresman and Co.

Computer Master 5

Linear Inequalities

To do this activity you need a grapher that can be used to draw inequalities. Use a separate pair of axes for each problem.

1. Graph $y > 3x + 1$. Determine which of the following are in the solution set of the inequality:

  a. $(-3, 3)$ _____

  b. $(4, -2)$ _____

  c. $(-1, -2)$ _____

2. Graph $y \geq 5x - 11$. Rescale to determine graphically which of the following points are in the solution set of the inequality:

  a. $(3, 6)$ _____

  b. $(4.4, 11)$ _____

  c. $(-2.25, -22.5)$ _____

3. Use the grapher to reproduce each inequality below. Record the inequality you used.

a.

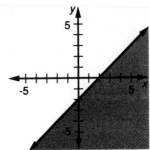

b.

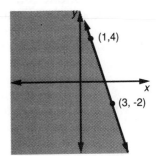

_____   _____

4. Use your grapher to draw four regions whose intersection forms the interior of a square and whose sides *are not* parallel to the coordinate axes. Record the inequalities used below, and sketch their graphs at the right.

_____   _____

_____   _____

Computer Master 5   (page 2)

Complete question 5 if your graphing software offers a cursor that can be moved along a graph or throughout the coordinate plane.

5. Graph $y \leq -\frac{2}{3}x - 8$. Move the cursor vertically to $y = 5$. Move the cursor horizontally until it coincides with a point on the line.

   a. What is the x-coordinate of the point?   _____

   b. For what values of x is $(x, -5)$ in the solution set of the inequality?   _____

   c. For what values of x is $(x, -5)$ not in the solution set of the inequality?   _____

6. Graph $y < 1 - 4x$. Find the solution set of the inequality $9 < 1 - 4x$ graphically. Solve the inequality algebraically to check your answer.

_____

7. To foster parity among its teams, the National Basketball Association imposes a "salary cap" on each team. Suppose the cap is $6.0 million and the New York Knicks have all but two players under contracts totaling $3.25 million. The value to the team of one remaining player is judged 1.5 times the value of the other. Set the grapher limits to $0 \leq x \leq 5$ along each axis and graph the inequality $y \leq 6.0 - 2.5x$ where x is the salary of the less valuable player and y is the amount already committed to signed players.

   a. Explain how the graph can be used to determine whether the Knicks will be under the cap if they sign the less valuable player for $1.25 million.

   _____

   b. Use the graph to determine the maximum amount that the Knicks can pay the less valuable player (to the nearest tenth of a million).

   _____

   c. The league also imposes a minimum salary level per team of $4.0 million. Rewrite the inequality, graph it, and use the graph to find the minimum amount the Knicks could pay the less valuable player (to the nearest tenth of a million).

   _____

Computer Master 6

Perpendicular Lines

Use a computer grapher to draw the lines in this activity. Do each problem on a separate pair of axes. Scale the pair of axes the same number of units.

1. Graph the line $y = 2x + 3$ (Use $f(x) = 2x + 3$). On the same pair of axes graph $y = 2x - 5$, $y = -2x + 3$, $y = \frac{1}{2}x + 3$ and $y = -\frac{1}{2}x + 3$.

   a. Which of the lines appears to be perpendicular to the first line? _____

   b. Compare the slopes of the perpendicular lines. Describe their relationship in words.

   _____

2. Graph the line $y = -\frac{2}{3}x$

   a. What is the slope of the line? _____

   b. What is the slope of a line perpendicular to this line? _____

   c. Write an equation and graph a line perpendicular to $y = -\frac{2}{3}x$. _____

   d. Write an equation and graph another line perpendicular to $y = -\frac{2}{3}x$. _____

   e. What is an equation for any line perpendicular to the given line? _____

3. Graph the line $y = -5x + 1$.

   a. What is the equation of a line that also has 1 as its y-intercept and is perpendicular to the given line? _____

   b. Draw the graph for the equation to check that the lines are perpendicular.

4. a. Graph the line passing through $(0, 0)$ and $(3, -4)$. What is an equation for this line? _____

   b. Graph the image of the line rotated 90° about the origin. What is an equation for this line? _____

Computer Master 6   (page 2)

5. a. Graph the line whose equation is
$y = -\dfrac{1}{3}x + 3.$

_____

b. Graph the image of the line rotated 90° about
the origin. What is an equation for this line?   _____

6. Graph the lines $y = x + 7$, $y = x - 3$, $y = -x$, $y = -x + 7$. True or
false: The lines intersect to form a rectangle. Justify your answer.

_____

7. The vertices of one side of a rectangle are (2, 8) and (5, 2). The opposite
side passes through the origin. Graph the four lines that determine the
rectangle. Record their equations.

_____

8. Find and write four equations for lines that intersect to form a square.

_____

9. a. Graph the lines $y = x$, $y = -4x + 5$, and $y = 3x + 12$ to make a
triangle.

b. Rescale to determine the coordinates of each
vertex.   _____

c. Graph and find an equation for the altitude to the side defined by
$y = 3x + 12.$

_____

Computer Master 6 (for use with Lesson 4-8)
Advanced Algebra © Scott, Foresman and Co.

Computer Master 7
Solving Systems of Equations Using Graphs

A computer grapher can be used to solve systems of equations graphically. For each system, graph the equations on the same set of axes. Then find the coordinates of the point(s) of intersection. It may be necessary to rescale to find some solutions.

In 1 and 2, each system has one solution and both coordinates of that point are integers. Graph the systems and find their solutions:

1. $y = 4x - 5$
$y = x - 5$

2. $y = 2x^2$
$y = -4x - 2$

Solution: _____

Solution: _____

3. The system $y = -\dfrac{12}{x}$ and $y = -.5x + 1$ has
two solutions and both coordinates of each point
of intersection are integers. Find the solutions.   _____

In 4 and 5, approximate to the nearest tenth the coordinates of all intersections in the solution set of the system.

4. $y = 3x - 4$
$y = -5x - 16$

5. $y = -x^2$
$y = -\dfrac{12}{x^2}$

Solution: _____

Solution: _____

In 6 and 7, graph each system and identify the system as consistent or inconsistent. If the system is consistent, find its solution. Round both coordinates to the nearest integer.

6. $y = 5x - 9$
$y = 3 + \dfrac{11}{2}x$

7. $y = x^2$
$y = 2x - 2$

Solution: _____

Solution: _____

8. In a free market economy, prices in the short run are determined by supply and demand. The equilibrium price is the price at which supply equals demand. Using the tables below, write equations for demand and supply, set the scale limits along each axis from 0 to 5, graph the equations, and find the solution. What is the equilibrium price of fish to the nearest cent? About how many tons of fish will be sold?

Demand for Fish				Supply of Fish		
tons/fish	5	3	1	tons/fish	1	2	3
price/lb	$2.00	$2.50	$3.00	price/lb	$2.00	$2.50	$3.00

Computer Master 7   (page 2)

9. Larry and Carla have 180 ft of fencing to construct three adjoining rectangular pens for their dogs, as shown at the right. Each pen must have an area of 150 sq. ft.

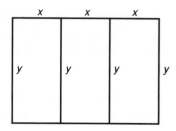

a. Write a system of equations which models the above conditions.

_____

b. Graph both equations in part **a** on the same set of axes. Estimate to the nearest tenth the coordinates of the points of intersection of the two curves.

(_____, _____) and (_____, _____)

c. What are the possible dimensions of the individual pens?

width (x) _____ and length (y) _____

width (x) _____ and length (y) _____

Computer Master 7 (for use with Lesson 5-2)
Advanced Algebra © Scott, Foresman and Co.

Computer Master 8
Linear Programming

To do the linear programming problems in this activity, it is best to have a
computer grapher that can graph inequalities. However, you can still do the
problems by graphing the related equations and visualizing them as
inequalities. Many graphers also require that equations and inequalities be
solved for y in order to be graphed. ($ax + by = c$ must be changed to its
equivalent form $y = \dfrac{c - ax}{b}$.)

> Disk Drive High School has $36,000 to spend on no more than 60 computers
> that can be accommodated in their two new computer labs. A Peach computer
> costs $750 and a Little Red computer costs $500. The lab teacher estimates that
> the average use of a Peach computer would be 25 hours per week and a Little
> Red 16 hours per week. The school wants to maximize the number of hours of
> computer usage.

1. Set the limits on your grapher from 0 to 100 along each axis. Let x and y
   be the number of Peach and Little Red computers, respectively.

   a. Graph $x + y \leq 60$. Explain the meaning of this inequality.

   _____

   b. Graph $750x + 500y \leq 36000$. Explain the meaning of this inequality.

   _____

   c. Let the usage formula be $u = 25x + 16y$ where u is the total number of
   hours that all the computers are used weekly. Draw lines for these
   values of u: 1440, 1320, 1200, 1080 and 960. Which lines intersect the

   feasible region? _____ Which ones intersect the

   feasible region at a vertex? _____ Of the lines that
   intersect the feasible region at a vertex, which has the greatest value

   of u? _____

   d. Find the coordinates of the vertex of the
   feasible region that maximizes computer
   usage. How many of each type of computer
   should be purchased?   _____

2. Before the computers can be ordered, the price of a Little Red computer
   drops to $450. Revise the inequality for the total cost and graph it on the
   same set of axes as the inequality $x + y \leq 60$.

   a. Find the coordinates of the vertices of the feasible region.

   _____

Computer Master 8   (page 2)

b. Graph $u = 25x + 16y$ for these values of u: 1260, 1230, 1200. Which line represents the number of hours the computers would be used? Explain why.

_____

_____

c. How many of each type of computer should now be purchased?

_____

3. Suppose the school board decides to cut computer lab funding to $27,000 and computer lab capacity to no more than 50 computers. Rewrite and graph the inequalities (using the new price for Little Red).

a. Find the coordinates of the vertices of the feasible region.

_____

b. Find the vertex that represents maximum computer usage by drawing lines with various values of u in $u = 25x + 16y$.

How many of each type of computer should be purchased under these new conditions?   _____

About how many hours will they be used each week?   _____

4. Suppose the price of a Little Red computer had not dropped. Do problem 3 again using the original price of Little Red and find the number of each type of computer that would be purchased.   _____

5. Based on what you have observed, explain how the relationship between the ratio of the estimated average number of hours of use of each computer and the ratio of the prices of the computers affects the number of each type of computer to be purchased.   _____

Computer Master 9

Applications of Quadratics

When a ball is thrown directly upward, its height at time t is determined by the formula

$$h = -\frac{1}{2}gt^2 + v_0t + h_0$$

where g is a gravitational constant, v_0 is the initial velocity of the ball, and h_0 is the ball's initial height. Near the surface of the earth, the value of g is about 32 ft/sec^2 or 9.8 m/sec^2.

1. Suppose a ball is thrown upward at 80 ft/sec from the ground level.

    a. What equation gives the height of the ball at
       time t?   _____

    b. Graph the equation in part **a** using a computer grapher. Set the window
       to $0 \le x \le 10$ and $0 \le y \le 100$.

    c. According to the graph, what is the
       approximate height of the ball after 1 second?   _____

    d. According to the equation, how high is the
       ball after 1 second?   _____

    e. After about how many seconds is the ball 80
       feet high?   _____

    f. About how many seconds does it take for the
       ball to reach its maximum height?   _____

    g. What is the maximum height attained by the
       ball?   _____

    h. For how many seconds is the ball in the air?   _____

2. Suppose the initial upward velocity of a second ball is half that of the ball
   in Question 1. This ball is also thrown from ground level.

    a. Write an equation for the height h of the ball
       at time t.   _____

    b. Graph the equation in part **a** on the same
       pair of axes used in Question 1.

    c. Is the second ball in the air half as long as the
       first ball?   _____

If not, how does the time spent in the air by the second ball compare to the time spent in the air by the first? _____

d. Does the second ball go half as high as the first ball? _____

If not, how does the maximum height of the second ball compare to the maximum height of the first? _____

3. Mt. Everest, with a height of about 8800 m, is the highest peak in the world. Suppose a model rocket is launched straight up from the top of Mt. Everest at an initial velocity of 36 m/sec.

   a. Write an equation for the height h of the rocket at time t. _____

   b. Graph the equation from part **a** for $t \geq 0$. (adjust the window so you can see the entire portion of the graph in the first quadrant.)

   c. After 2 seconds how high is the rocket

      i. according to the graph? _____

      ii. according to the equation? _____

   d. What is the approximate maximum height above sea level attained by the rocket? _____

   e. After about how many seconds is the maximum height attained? _____

   f. Assuming there are no barriers to the rocket's fall, after about how much time would the rocket

      i. be back at the height of 8800 m? _____

      ii. hit sea level? _____

NAME _____

Computer Master 9 (page 3)

4. Experiment with the computer grapher to find the initial velocity of a ball thrown upward from a height of 14 ft if the maximum height attained by the ball is 50 feet.

Record an equation and graph that justify your answer.

equation: _____

initial velocity: _____

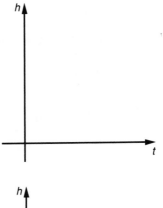

5. Experiment with the computer grapher to find the initial velocity of a ball thrown upward from ground level if the ball is in the air for 4 seconds.

Record an equation and graph that justify your answer.

equation: _____

initial velocity: _____

Computer Master 10
The Graph Translation Theorem

Use a computer grapher to answer each of the following questions. Attach hard copies from your printer or handsketches of the graphs made for each question. Recall that the equation of any parabola with its vertex at the origin is $y = ax^2$. Any other parabola in the coordinate plane with a vertical axis of symmetry is a translation image of a parabola with its vertex at the origin.

1. a. On one set of axes graph the four equations and identify for each the equation of the axis of symmetry and the coordinates of the vertex.

Equation	Equation of Axis of Symmetry	Coordinates of Vertex
$y = x^2$	$x = 0$	
$y = (x - 3)^2$		
$y = x^2 + 7$		$(0, 7)$
$y = (x - 3)^2 + 7$		

b. Without graphing predict the coordinates of the vertex of the graph of $y = (x - 1)^2 + 7$. _____

Check your result by graphing.

c. In general, the graph of $y - k = (x - h)^2$ or $y = (x - h)^2 + k$

represents a translation of _____ units horizontally and _____ units vertically from the graph of $y = x^2$. So, $y = (x - h)^2 + k$ has as its axis

of symmetry the line _____ , and as its vertex the

point _____ .

2. a. Graph the equations below and complete the chart.

Equation	Equation of Axis of Symmetry	Coordinates of Vertex
$y = -2x^2$		
$y = -2(x + 5)^2$		
$y = -2x^2 + 1$		
$y = -2(x + 5)^2 + 1$		

b. Without graphing predict what the graph of $y = -2(x + 5)^2 - 4$ will look like in comparison to the graph of $y = -2x^2$.

_____

Check your prediction by graphing $y = -2x^2$ and $y = -2(x + 5)^2 - 4$ on the same set of axes.

Computer Master 10 (for use with Lesson 6-4)
Advanced Algebra © Scott, Foresman and Co.

Computer Master 10   (page 2)

3. Refer to the graphs made in Questions 1 and 2. Consider an equation of the form $y - k = a(x - h)^2$ or its equivalent $y = a(x - h)^2 + k$.

   a. The graph has an axis of symmetry with an equation

   _____ , and a vertex with coordinates

   _____ .

   b. The graph opens up when _____ ; it opens down

   when _____ .

   c. The graph is a translation of h units horizontally and k units vertically

   from the graph of _____ .

4. a. Graph $y = .2x^2$ on the window $-5 \le x \le 5$ and $-5 \le y \le 5$.

   b. Write an equation for the image of this
      parabola under the translation $T_{-1,-3}$.   _____

   c. Check your answer to part b by graphing the equation on the same set
      of axes used for part a.

5. Graph a parabola congruent to $y = -5x^2$ with
   vertex at $(-2, 4)$. Check your work using the
   computer grapher.   _____

6. Graph $y = -\frac{1}{2}x^2$. Graph its image

   under $T_{8,3}$. Check your work using the computer
   grapher.   _____

7. Graph $y = 3x^2$. On the same axis graph $y = x^2 + 3$, $y = 3x^2 + 12x + 16$, $y = \frac{x^2}{3}$, and $y = -3x^2 + 2x$. Which of these four parabolas
   appear to be translation images of $y = 3x^2$?   _____

8. a. Graph $y = 2x^2$ and $y = 2x^2 + 24x + 74$, its image under a translation
      $T_{h,k}$.

   b. Find the coordinates of the vertex of the
      second parabola.   _____

   c. Find the values of h and k that define the
      translation.   _____

Computer Master 10   (page 3)

9. a. Graph $y = \dfrac{4}{x}$. The asymptotes of the hyperbola are $x = 0$ and $y = 0$.

   b. Draw the graph $y = \dfrac{4}{x} + 7$.

   c. What are equations for its asymptotes?   _____

   d. Is the second hyperbola a translation image

      of the first? _____ If so, what translation
      maps $y = \dfrac{4}{x}$ onto $y = \dfrac{4}{x} + 7$?   _____

10. a. Graph $y = -\dfrac{12}{x}$.

   b. Write an equation for its image under $T_{2,-3}$.
      Check your work using the computer
      grapher.   _____

11. a. Check $y = \dfrac{8}{x^2}$. Find an equation for its image
      under $T_{-5,-3}$. Check your work using the
      computer grapher.

Computer Master 11
Roots of Quadratics

In the equation $ax^2 + bx + c = 0$, the number of real roots and their values can be determined using the graph of $y = ax^2 + bx + c$. The roots of the quadratic equation are the x-intercepts of the graph. Use a computer grapher to do each problem on a separate pair of axes.

1. Graph $y = x^2 + 3x - 10$.

    a. At how many points does the graph intersect
       the x-axis? _____

    b. How many real roots does $x^2 + 3x - 10 = 0$
       have? _____

    c. What are the coordinates of the x-intercepts
       of the graph? _____

    d. What are the real roots of the equation
       $x^2 + 3x - 10 = 0$? _____

2. Use the appropriate graph to determine the number of real roots and their values for each of the quadratic equations below. Round all non-integral roots to the nearest tenth.

    a. $2x^2 + 3x + 3 = 0$ _____

    b. $-x^2 + 8x - 9 = 0$ _____

    c. $x^2 + 49 = -14x$ _____

3. A projectile shot from a cannon at a 30° angle from the horizontal with an initial velocity of 1000 feet per second follows a path described by the formula $y = .57x - .00002x^2$. Determine whether the projectile will undershoot, hit, or overshoot a target that is a half-mile away. Justify your answer.

_____

4. Graph $y = ax^2 + bx + c$ for $a = 2$, $b = -8$, and $x = 9$.

    a. How many roots does the equation
       $2x^2 - 8x + 9 = 0$ have? _____

    b. Compute the value of the discriminant
       $b^2 - 4ac$. Is the discriminant greater than,
       equal to, or less than 0? _____

    c. Change the value of c from 9 to -9 and
       graph the new equation on the same axes.
       How many real roots does $2x^2 - 8x - 9 = 0$
       have? _____

Computer Master 11   (page 2)

d. Compute the value of the discriminant for the new equation. How does it compare to 0 now? _____

e. Find the value of c for which the discriminant equals 0. Graph the corresponding equation, $y = 2x^2 - 8x + 8$. _____

f. Either print a hard copy of the three graphs on the screen or copy the graphs on graph paper. How are the graphs of the three equations related?

_____

_____

g. Make a conjecture about the axis of symmetry of the graph of any equation of the form $y = 2x^2 - 8x + c$. Test your conjecture on some new values of c. Write a paragraph stating your conjecture, how you tested it, and what conclusion you drew.

_____

_____

_____

5. Graph $y = ax^2 + bx + c$ for $a = 2$, $b = 13$, and $c = 18$.

a. How many roots does the equation $2x^2 + 13x + 18 = 0$ have? _____

b. Using the discriminant $b^2 - 4ac$, change the value of b so that the equation will have one real root. Graph the new equation on the same set of axes. _____

c. Does changing the value of b affect the graph in the same way as changing the value of c? _____

d. Experiment with different values of b in the equation $y = 2x^2 + bx + c$. Write an equation for the axis of symmetry of $y = 2x^2 + bx + 18$. (Hint: The equation is related to only two of 2, b, and 18.) _____

e. In general, the equation of the axis of symmetry of $y = ax^2 + bx + c$ is related to only two of a, b, and c. Experiment with various values of a, b, and c to determine this equation. Write a paragraph summarizing your procedures and your conclusions. Attach graphs to justify your conclusions.

_____

_____

_____

Computer Master 11 (for use with Lesson 6-7)
Advanced Algebra © Scott, Foresman and Co.

Computer Master 12

Using Functions in BASIC

BASIC has a number of built-in functions that perform both arithmetic and non-arithmetic tasks. These are used by an abbreviation of the name of the function followed by an argument enclosed in parentheses. Functions can also be defined using the DEF FN command and then used in the same way as built-in functions.

1. Use the PRINT command with the abbreviation to evaluate each built-in numerical function for the following values.

$$25, 87, 0, .0036, -10, -.0036$$

For example, to do the first one type PRINT SQR(25). Do not type a line number. Then describe the function in words, including any apparent restrictions on the domain of x.

a. SQR(x) _____

b. ABS(x) _____

c. SGN(x) _____

2. The following BASIC program contains a user-defined function:

```
10   DEF FN F(X) = 3 * X
20   FOR X = 1 TO 6
30     PRINT X, FN F(X)
40   NEXT X
50   END
```

a. RUN the program. Record the output.

_____

b. Describe the output in words.

_____

3. Refer to the program in Question 2.

a. Change lines 10 and 20 to print tables of values of the following functions for integer x values from 0 to 10. Attach a hard copy of your output, or a copy made by hand.

square numbers _____

the powers of 2 _____

b. Refer to your output. List the integers on the domain $0 \le x \le 10$ for which each statement is true.

$x < 2$ _____ $x = 2$ _____ $x > 2$ _____

Computer Master 12   (page 2)

4. a. Revise the original program in Question 2 to print a table of values for the quadratic function $f(x) = 4x^2 - 9x + 3$ using integers from -5 to 5 as values of x.

_____

b. Refer to your table.

   i. Evaluate $f(1)$.   _____

   ii. For what value of x is $f(x) = 1$?   _____

   iii. Which is larger: $f(-5)$ or $f(5)$?   _____

c. Sketch a graph of the function $y = f(x)$. Name the curve, and list some of its properties.

_____

5. Revise lines 10 and 20 in the program in Question 2 to study $f(x) = 2x^2 - 13x - 24$. Print a table of functional values using integers from -10 to 10 as values of x.

a. Does the equation $2x^2 - 13x - 24 = 0$ have any *integral* roots between -10 and 10? If so, state them.   _____

b. Revise line 20 as follows: FOR X = -10 TO 10 STEP .5. RUN the program. What is another solution of the equation $f(x) = 0$?   _____

c. Show that your answers to parts **a** and **b** are correct by solving $2x^2 - 13x - 24 = 0$ using the quadratic formula.   _____

6. The argument of a function may itself include a variable.

a. Define the function on line 10 as $f(x) = 5x - 8$, and print a table of values on the domain $0 \leq x \leq 6$. Record your results.

_____

b. Change line 30 to PRINT X, FN F(2 * X). RUN the program. Record the output. Are the values of $F(2x)$ twice as large as those of the original $f(x)$ in part **a**?   _____

If not, how do they compare?   _____

c. Without changing lines 10 or 20, how would you change line 30 so that the functional values printed will be 12, 17, 22, 27, 32, 37, and 42?

_____

Computer Master 13

Composition of Functions

Before doing this activity, find out if your computer grapher can be used to do compositions of functions. (This may be termed *user-defined functions* in your grapher.) If not, you will have to find each composite yourself before graphing it. (For example, if $f(x) = 5x - 1$ and $g(x) = \dfrac{1}{x^2}$, then $f(g(x)) = 5\left(\dfrac{1}{x^2}\right) - 1$. Simplifying is not necessary.) Use a separate pair of axes for each problem.

1. Let $f(x) = 2x - 1$ and $g(x) = x + 4$.

    a. Graph $f(x)$ and $g(x)$ on the same set of axes. Describe the graphs and their relationship.

    _____

    b. Graph $f(g(x))$ and $g(f(x))$ on the same set of axes. Describe the graphs and their relationship.

    _____

2. Without graphing, make a conjecture about the relationship between the graphs of $f(g(x))$ and $g(f(x))$ if $f(x) = 3x + 1$ and $g(x) = -2x - 3$. Test your conjecture by graphing each composite function.

_____

_____

3. Let $f(x) = \dfrac{1}{x}$ and $g(x) = x + 3$.

    a. Graph $f(x)$ and $g(x)$ on the same set of axes. Describe the graphs and any restrictions on their domains.

    _____

    b. Graph $f(g(x))$. Compare its graph with the graphs of $f(x)$ and $g(x)$.

    _____

    c. Graph $g(f(x))$ and $f(g(x))$ on the same set of axes. Describe the graphs of the two composite functions and their relationship.

    _____

    d. Describe any restrictions on the domains of $f(g(x))$ and $g(f(x))$.

    _____

Computer Master 13 (page 2)

4. In each of the following, draw the graphs of f(x) and g(x) and describe each. Then compare the graphs of f(g(x)) and g(f(x)):

   a. $f(x) = x^2$; $g(x) = x - 5$

   _____

   b. $f(x) = \dfrac{2}{x}$; $g(x) = 2x^2$

   _____

   c. $f(x) = \dfrac{1}{x}$; $g(x) = \dfrac{3}{x}$

   _____

   d. $f(x) = \dfrac{1}{x^2}$; $g(x) = 3x^2$

   _____

5. Use your results from problem 4 and draw new graphs if necessary to complete the table below. In each box in the table, write the type of graph f(g(x)) will produce.

		f(x)			
		Line	Parabola	Hyperbola	Inverse Square
	Line	_____	_____	_____	_____
	Parabola	_____	_____	_____	_____
g(x)	Hyperbola	_____	_____	_____	_____
	Inverse square	_____	_____	_____	_____

6. The table above is symmetrical. However, that does not imply that composition of functions is commutative. Explain why.

   _____

7. Make a conjecture about the graph of the composition of an inverse square function and a cubic function. Using $f(x) = \dfrac{1}{x^2}$ and $g(x) = x^3$, graph f(g(x)) and g(f(x)).

   _____

Computer Master 13 (for use with Lesson 7-3)
Advanced Algebra © Scott, Foresman and Co.

Computer Master 14
Step Functions

The INT function in BASIC denotes the greatest integer function. It outputs the largest integer less than or equal to a given number. INT is useful in defining step functions.

1. The cost C of shipping a package from New York City to Los Angeles via a certain delivery service is $C = 1.49 + .42[W]$, where W is the weight of the package.

   a. Complete the following program that calculates the shipping charges for small packages.

   ```
   10   PRINT "WEIGHT", "COST"
   20   FOR W = .1 TO 3 STEP .1
   30     C = _____
   40     PRINT W,C
   50   NEXT W
   ```

   b. RUN the program. How much does it cost to ship a package weighing 2.9 lb?   _____

   c. How should line 20 be modified so the program finds shipping costs for weights up to 10 lb. in increments of .5 lb?   _____

   d. Use the program in part c to find the possible weight of a package that costs $4.01 to ship.   _____

2. Consider the program below.

   ```
    5   PRINT "TO STOP THE PROGRAM TYPE A
         NEGATIVE NUMBER"
   10   INPUT "A NON-NEGATIVE NUMBER"; X
   20   IF X < 0 THEN GOTO 60
   30   DEF FN F(X) = 10 * INT(X + 5) / 10
   40   PRINT "F(X) = "; FN F(X)
   50   GOTO 10
   60   END
   ```

   a. RUN the program using 3, 4.9, 8.27, 0.6, 42.92, 368, and 512 as inputs. Describe the value of FN F(X) in words.

   _____

   b. Change line 30 to the following:

   ```
   30   DEF FN F(X) = 100 * INT((X + 50) / 100)
   ```

   RUN the program again using the same data as in part a. Describe the output of the program.

   _____

Computer Master 14   (page 2)

c. Modify the program so it rounds the numbers input to the nearest thousand. Record your modifications.

_____

Record the numbers you used to test your program.

_____

3. In the "4-point" grading scale used by many high schools and colleges, letter grades are assigned points (A-4; B-3; C-2; D-1; F-0). Dr. Tuff uses the function f(x) defined below to convert any numerical score to its grade-point equivalent, 4, 3, 2, 1, or 0.

$$\text{FN F(X)} = 4 - \text{INT} ((100 - X) / 7)$$

a. Revise the program in Question 2 to convert scores in Professor Tuff's class to grade-point equivalents.

b. RUN the program by entering various scores between 0 and 100. Determine the scale Dr. Tuff uses to determine letter grades for her mathematics class.

c. Modify this program so it converts scores from a different 0 to 100 scale used by a teacher you know to the 0 to 4 scale. Record your program and the grading scale it converts.

4. Tables used for federal income tax are step functions. The portion of the Form 1040-1988 Tax Table shown below is used to determine the tax on taxable incomes between $35,000 and $36,000:

If line 37 (taxable income) is—		And you are—			
At least	But less than	Single	Married filing jointly	Married filing sepa-rately	Head of a house-hold
			Your tax is—		
35,000					
35,000	35,050	7,487	5,940	7,873	6,700
35,050	35,100	7,501	5,954	7,887	6,714
35,100	35,150	7,515	5,968	7,901	6,728
35,150	35,200	7,529	5,982	7,915	6,742
35,200	35,250	7,543	5,996	7,929	6,756
35,250	35,300	7,557	6,010	7,943	6,770
35,300	35,350	7,571	6,024	7,957	6,784
35,350	35,400	7,585	6,038	7,971	6,798
35,400	35,450	7,599	6,052	7,985	6,812
35,450	35,500	7,613	6,066	7,999	6,826
35,500	35,550	7,627	6,080	8,013	6,840
35,550	35,600	7,641	6,094	8,027	6,854
35,600	35,650	7,655	6,108	8,041	6,868
35,650	35,700	7,669	6,122	8,055	6,882
35,700	35,750	7,683	6,136	8,069	6,896
35,750	35,800	7,697	6,150	8,083	6,910
35,800	35,850	7,711	6,164	8,097	6,924
35,850	35,900	7,725	6,178	8,111	6,938
35,900	35,950	7,739	6,192	8,125	6,952
35,950	36,000	7,753	6,206	8,141	6,966
36,000					

Computer Master 14 (for use with Lesson 7-4)
Advanced Algebra © Scott, Foresman and Co.

Computer Master 14   (page 3)

a. Write a program to determine the tax for a single person with a taxable income of at least $35,000 but less than $36,000. Verify your work by using various taxable incomes within the domain of the function.

b. Modify the program and add a FOR . . . NEXT to make a table showing the tax on single persons with taxable incomes of at least $36,000 but less than $37,000 (assume the same increments as between $35,000 and $36,000).

c. Modify the program to print a table showing the tax on a married couple filing jointly with taxable income of at least $36,000 but less than $37,000.

Computer Master 15

Absolute Value and Powering

Use your computer grapher to do each problem on a separate set of axes.

1. Graph $y = |x|$. On the same set of axes graph each of the following and compare it to the graph of $y = |x|$ in terms of a translation $T_{h,k}$:

   a. $y = |x| - 2$ $h =$ _____; $k =$ _____

   b. $y = |x + 5|$ $h =$ _____; $k =$ _____

2. Reproduce each of the following. Record the function graphed.

   a.
   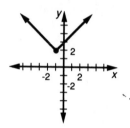

   b.
   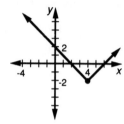

   _____   _____

3. Graph $y = |x|$. On the same set of axes:

   a. Graph $y = |3x|$ and $y = |-5x|$. Describe the effect of a on the graph of $y = |ax|$.

   _____

   b. Graph $y = 3|x|$ and $y = -5|x|$. Compare and contrast the graphs of $y = |ax|$ and $y = a|x|$.

   _____

4. Reproduce each of the following with your computer grapher. Record the functions graphed.

   a.
   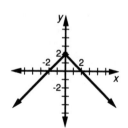

   b.
   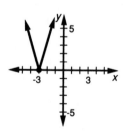

   _____   _____

5. Graph $y = x^3$. On the same axes, graph $y = -x^3$ and $y = 4x^3$. Describe the effect of a on the graph of $y = ax^3$.

   _____

Computer Master 15 (for use with Lesson 7-5)
Advanced Algebra © Scott, Foresman and Co.

Computer Master 15   (page 2)

6. Write an equation g for the image of the function f under the translation, then graph both the function and its image.

a. $f(x) = x^4$ under $T_{3,0}$ _____

b. $f(x) = x^5$ under $T_{-2,-1}$ _____

c. True or false: "The image of a power function under a translation is congruent to the preimage."   _____

7. The graph shaped like the one at the right contains the points (2, 17), (4, 1), and (6, 17).

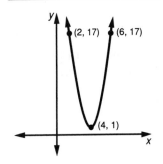

a. Find a quadratic function which passes through these points.   _____

b. Find an equation of the form $f(x) = a(x - h)^4 + k$ containing these points.   _____

c. Are the graphs of the two functions in parts **a** and **b** congruent?   _____

If not, which rises more quickly (has a larger rate of change) between $x = 4$ and $x = 5$? (You may need to rescale to answer this question.)

_____

8. a. Graph $f(x) = |x|$; $g(x) = x^3$ on the same axes. Then describe the values in their domains for which the following are true.

$f(x) > g(x)$ _____

$f(x) = g(x)$ _____

$f(x) < g(x)$ _____

b. Consider $f(x) = |x|$ and $g(x) = (x + 4)^2 - 2$. For what values of x does $f(x) = g(x)$? Check your answer(s) by substitution.

_____

c. Solve graphically: $-|x| = x^2 - 12$, and check your answer(s) by substitution.

_____

Computer Master 16

Inverses

**This activity can be done with any computer grapher. However, if your
grapher can do inverses of functions, you can also use it to verify your work.
Do each problem on a separate pair of axes.**

1. On the same axes graph $y = 2x + 2$ and $y = \dfrac{1}{2}x - 1$. Are the two

   functions inverses? Explain why or why not in terms of the relationship of
   the two functions to the line $y = x$. (If your grapher does inverses, graph
   the inverse of one function, then compare it to the graph of the other
   function.)

   _____

2. Use the grapher as you did in problem 1 to determine whether the
   functions in each pair are inverses:

   a. $y = x + 4$ and $y = -x - 4$ _____

   b. $y = \dfrac{2}{x - 1}$ and $y = \dfrac{2}{x} + 1$ _____

   c. $y = \dfrac{2}{5}x + 1$ and $y = \dfrac{5}{2}x - \dfrac{2}{5}$ _____

   d. $y = 5x - 3$ and $y = \dfrac{x + 3}{5}$ _____

3. Graph $y = 3x - 6$. Find the equation of the
   line that is the reflection of $y = 3x - 6$ over
   $y = x$. Graph the equation.   _____

4. Find the equation of the inverse of the linear
   function shown in the drawing below. Graph
   both the function and its inverse on the same
   set of axes.   _____

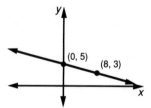

5. Graph $y = \dfrac{3}{x + 1}$ and its inverse on the same

   set of axes. What is the equation of the inverse?   _____

Computer Master 16 (for use with Lessons 7-6 and 7-7)
Advanced Algebra © Scott, Foresman and Co.

Computer Master 16   (page 2)

6. Set the limits of the grapher from -10 to 10 along each axes. Graph $f(x) = 2x^2$.

    a. Explain how to use the horizontal line test to decide whether the inverse of $f(x)$ is a function.

    _____

    b. Describe how the domain of $f(x)$ must be limited in order for its inverse to be a function.

    _____

    c. Set the limits on the x-axis to reflect the domain you gave for part **b.** Graph the inverse of $f(x)$. What is the equation for the inverse of $f(x)$?   _____

7. Graph each function and use the horizontal line test to determine whether its inverse is a function. If it fails the test, describe how the domain of $f(x)$ must be limited so its inverse will also be a function. Set the limits on the grapher accordingly and graph both $f(x)$ and $f^{-1}(x)$ on the same axes to verify your work.

    a. $f(x) = (x - 5)^2$ _____

    b. $f(x) = \dfrac{1}{4}x^2$ _____

Computer Master 17
Compound Interest

The following BASIC program can be used to compute the balance in an account at the end of T years given P, the original amount invested and R, the annual rate of interest.

```
 5   PRINT "PRINCIPAL, ANNUAL RATE, NO. OF YEARS";
10   INPUT P, R, T
15   PRINT "YEAR", "BALANCE"
20   FOR C = 1 TO T
30     LET P = P * (1 + R)
40     PRINT C, P
50   NEXT C
60   END
```

1. a. Is the formula in line 30 explicit or recursive?   _____

   b. Use 5000, .07, 10 as input to determine the end-of-year balances in an account in which $5000 is placed for 10 years at 7% per year compounded annually.   _____

   c. How much interest is earned in the first year?   _____

   d. How much interest is earned in the tenth year?   _____

   e. What is the total interest earned in ten years?   _____

   f. After how many years will the balance be about $7500?   _____

   g. RUN the program again using a larger value of T. After how many years will the balance be about $15000?   _____

2. "College Sure" is an investment plan that offers flexible interest rates based on the rate of increase in college tuitions. The concept is to guarantee that parents will be able to afford tuition costs when their child enters college. If tuition at State U. is currently $8000 and increasing on the average 10% each year, modify the program above to print a table of the estimated annual tuition for the next 18 years.

3. a. Use the program above to determine the number of years it takes to double an investment at 8% per year compounded annually (Use $P = 100$).   _____

   b. About how many years will it take to double an investment at 6% per year compounded annually?   _____

Computer Master 17 (for use with Lesson 8-2)
Advanced Algebra © Scott, Foresman and Co.

Computer Master 17   (page 2)

c. About how many years will it take to double
an investment at 4% compounded annually?   _____

d. Make a conjecture about the relationship between d, the number of
years it takes to double an investment, and r, the rate at which the
investment is compounded annually

_____

e. Test your conjecture on some other rate $r < .15$. Describe the results of
your test.

_____

4. An explicit formula to compute a balance given the principal P, annual
rate of interest R, the number of compounding periods per year N, and the
number of years T is $A = P\left(1\frac{R}{N}\right)^{NT}$. Change the following lines in the
program:

```
 5   PRINT "PRINCIPAL, ANNUAL RATE, # OF
            PERIODS/YR, # OF YRS";
10   INPUT P, R, N, T
30   LET A = P * (1 + R/N) ^ (N * T)
55   PRINT T, A
```

Delete line 40.

a. Find the balance after 3 years on $1000
invested at 6% compounded annually.   _____

b. semi-annually   _____

c. quarterly   _____

d. monthly   _____

e. daily (assume no leap years)   _____

f. How much more money is earned by
compounding daily rather than annually?   _____

5. a. Which is a better deal: investing money for one year at 7%
compounded annually or at 6% compounded monthly? Justify your
answer.

_____

b. How, if at all, does your answer to part **a** change if the investment is
made for 5 years rather than 1 year?

_____

Computer Master 18

Geometric Sequences

Consider the BASIC program below, which produces a table with terms of a geometric sequence:

```
10   FOR N = 1 TO 10
20      LET T = 5 * 4 ^ (N − 1)
30      PRINT N, T
40   NEXT N
50   END
```

1. a. RUN the program. How many lines of output
are produced?   _____

What is the last line printed?   _____

b. How should line 20 be revised so that the
computer prints values of T starting with 3,
12, 48, 192, . . . when the program is run?   _____

In 2–4, modify lines 10 and 20 so the program produces each of these geometric sequences:

2. The first 12 terms of 16, 32, 64, 128, 256, . . .   _____

3. The first 25 terms of 200, 20, 2, .2, .02, . . .   _____

4. The first 15 terms of a geometric sequence in
which the first term is −7 and each term is three
times the preceding term.   _____

5. a. Modify the program so that it prints the first
18 terms of the sequence 2, 6, 18, 54, . . .   _____

b. How many terms of the sequence are
between 10 and 100?   _____

c. How many terms are between 100 and 1000?   _____

d. How many terms are between 1000 and
10000?   _____

e. If k is any whole number, how many terms
are between 10^k and 10^{k+1}?   _____

Justify your answer.

_____

Computer Master 18   (page 2)

6. The population of Brazil in 1988 was 144,400,000 and its annual growth rate was 2.0%. In the same year the population of the United States was 246,100,000 and its growth rate was 0.7%. Assume the growth rates continue indefinitely, and that they are compounded annually. Round all populations to the nearest 100,000 in your answers.

   a. Modify the program so it prints the projected annual population of each country for each year in the period 1988–2000. What is the projected population for each country in the year 2000?

   _____

   b. In about how many years after 1988 will the population of Brazil be double its 1988 population?

   What will the population of the U.S. be that year?   _____

   c. In about what year will Brazil's population exceed that of the United States?

   _____

7. The following data about population density in the 20th century comes from the U.S. Bureau of the Census:

Year	1900	1920	1940	1960	1980
Population (per Sq. Mile)	21.5	29.9	37.2	50.6	64.0

   a. If the increase in population per square mile is modeled by a geometric sequence, what is the approximate constant ratio?   _____

   b. Use the constant ratio to estimate the population per square mile at the end of the 20th century and at the end of the 21st century.   _____

   c. Using a constant ratio that is 0.1 less than the ratio used in part b, how much different is the estimate for the year 2100?   _____

Computer Master 19

Exponential Growth and Decay

If your computer grapher can be used to graph exponential equations
$y = ab^x$, **use the grapher to do each problem below on a separate pair of**
axes.

1. With the limits of the graph set from -10 to 10 on each axis, use the
   grapher to draw $y = 5 \cdot 2^x$. Does the function intersect the x-axis or the
   y-axis? For each axis, either find the intercept or explain why the graph
   doesn't intersect that axis.

   _____

2. Change the limits of the graph to $-5 \le x \le 5$ and $0 \le y \le 200$. Then, for
   each item below, using the equation $y = 5 \cdot 2^x$, rescale to:

   a. find y if $x = 2$ _____

   b. find x if $y = 160$ _____

   c. find y if $x = -1$ _____

   d. approximate x to the nearest tenth when
       $y = 50$ _____

   e. approximate y to the nearest tenth when
       $x = 2.8$ _____

   (Check your answers to **a-c** without using a calculator or computer; use a
   calculator to check **d** and **e**.)

3. **a.** Graph $y = 2^x$, $y = (3.5)^x$, and $y = 10^x$ on
      the same set of axes. State the coordinates of
      one point the graphs have in common.   _____

   b. If $b > 1$, state the effect of b on the graph of $y = b^x$.

      _____

   c. Clear the screen. Graph $y = (.9)^x$, $y = (.5)^x$, and $y = (.125)^x$ on the
      same set of axes. If $0 < b < 1$, describe the graph of $y = b^x$.

      _____

4. **a.** Set the limits from -10 to 10 on each axis and graph $y = 2^x$, $y =$
      $3 \cdot 2^x$, and $y = 6 \cdot 2^x$. Describe in words the effect of a on the graph of
      $y = a(2)^x$.

      _____

   b. Graph $y = a(2)^x$ using other values of a including $a < 0$. What effect
      does the sign of a have on the graph of $y = a(2)^x$?

      _____

Computer Master 19   (page 2)

5. Graph the equation $y = 3^x$. Rescale to solve the equation $99 = 3^x$. (Round your answer to the nearest hundredth.)   _____

6. **a.** On the same set of axes, graph $y = 3 \cdot 8^x$ and $y = 8 \cdot 3^x$. Find the coordinates of the point at which the graphs intersect.   _____

   b. Clear the screen. On the same set of axes graph another pair of equations of the form $y = ab^x$ and $y = ba^x$, where a and b are both positive. Find the coordinates of the point of intersection.

   _____

   c. Make a conjecture about where the graph of $y = ab^x$ intersects that of $y = ba^x$ for any positive numbers a and b.

   _____

7. The Consumer Price Index (CPI) is the measure of the average change in prices of goods over time. Using 1967 as the base year (CPI = 100.0), the CPI in 1987 was 330.5. Inflation estimates can be made from the CPI using the exponential equation $y = 100(1 + r)^x$, where x is the number of years and r is the average annual rate of inflation. To approximate inflation in prices over the 20-year period 1967–1987:

   a. Set the limits to $-10 \leq x \leq 20$ and $0 \leq y \leq 500$. Graph $y = 100(1.07)^x$. Use the graph to find the CPI in 1987 if inflation had averaged 7% per year.   _____

   b. Comparing your answer to the actual CPI, explain whether annual inflation averaged more or less than 7%?   _____

   c. Vary the inflation rate in the equation to draw other graphs on the same axes in order to approximate the rate of inflation in food prices to the nearest 0.5%.   _____

Computer Master 20

Logarithms

The LOG function in BASIC is used to find the natural logarithm of a number, a concept which you will learn about soon. Common logarithms or logarithms to bases other than 10 can be approximated with the exponential equation $b^n = m$ in the program below:

```
10   LET B = 10
20   PRINT "BASE IS"; B
30   PRINT "NUMBER", "LOG"
40   FOR N = −5 TO 5 STEP 1
50     LET M = B ∧ N
60     PRINT M, N
70   NEXT N
80   END
```

1. Use the program in answering the following:

   a. RUN the program in order to complete the following statements.

     The common logarithm of 1 is _____ .

     The common logarithm of 10 is _____ .

     Therefore the common logarithm of any number between 1 and 10 is

     between _____ and _____ .

     Similarly, if a number is between .01 and .1, its common logarithm is

     between _____ and _____ .

   b. Change line 40 to: FOR N = 0 TO 1 STEP 0.1 and RUN the program. Find two consecutive numbers in the table such that one of them is greater than 6 and the other is less than 6. Find the common logarithm of each of those numbers.

     Based on this information, the common logarithm of 6 lies between

     _____ and _____ .

   c. Change line 40 to: FOR N = 0.7 TO 0.8 STEP 0.01 and RUN the program in order to complete the following statements.

     The common logarithm of 6 lies between _____ and _____ .

     To the nearest tenth, log 6 = _____ .

   d. Change line 40 again and use the program to approximate log 6 to the nearest hundredth. _____

Computer Master 20 (for use with Lessons 9-4 and 9-5)
Advanced Algebra © Scott, Foresman and Co.

Computer Master 20   (page 2)

    e. Use the program to approximate log 152 to
the nearest tenth.   _____

    f. Use the program to approximate log 0.5 to
the nearest tenth.   _____

    g. Use the program to solve $28 = 10^n$ for n to
the nearest tenth.   _____

2. Change the base in the program to 2. Use the program to:

    a. find $\log_2 64$ _____

    b. approximate $\log_2 14.2$ to the nearest
hundredth   _____

    c. approximate $\log_2 0.04$ to the nearest tenth   _____

    d. solve $2^n = 440$ (Round to the nearest tenth.)   _____

3. Use the program to do each problem. Round to the nearest tenth
whenever an answer is not exact.

    a. Find $\log_5 100$.   _____

    b. Find $\log_8 0.2$.   _____

    c. Solve $4^n = 0.25$.   _____

    d. Solve $\dfrac{1}{2} = 3^n$.   _____

    e. Find log 0.0035.   _____

    f. Solve $-0.8 = \log_6 x$.   _____

Computer Master 21

Graphing Logarithms

Many computer graphers do not accept logarithmic equations other than
natural logarithms. However, equations in logarithmic form can be changed to
exponential form: $y = \log_b(x)$ is the same as $x = b^y$, and the inverse function
$y = b^x$ can be graphed. If your grapher can do inverses of functions, use it to
graph the inverse of $y = b^x$, which would be the original logarithmic equation.

1. a. Write the common logarithm $y = \log(x)$ in
exponential form.   _____

   b. Write the inverse function of your answer to
part **a** and graph it using the interval -1 to 1.   _____

   c. Use your computer grapher to graph the inverse of your answer to
part **b.**

2. Use the graphs obtained in **1b** and **1c** to:

   a. find the value of log (1).   _____

   b. approximate log (3.2) to the nearest tenth.   _____

   c. approximate $10^{0.5}$ to the nearest tenth.   _____

   d. What is the relationship between the two problems posed in **b** and **c**,
and their solutions?

_____

3. Use the steps from problem **1a-c** to graph the following. For each equation
give the x-intercept.

   a. $y = \log(x)$ x-intercept = _____

   b. $y = \log_2(x)$ x-intercept = _____

   c. $y = \log_4(x)$ x-intercept = _____

   d. $y = \log_7(x)$ x-intercept = _____

   e. What conjecture can you make about the x-intercept for the equation
$y = \log_b(x)$ for any base b?

_____

Computer Master 21 (for use with Lessons 9-4 and 9-5)
Advanced Algebra © Scott, Foresman and Co.

Computer Master 21   (page 2)

4. a. Graph $y = \log_2(x)^3$

  b. Graph $y = \log_3(x)$

    Find the value of y for $x = 3$ _____ and

                           $x = 9$ _____

  c. Graph $y = \log_3(x)^2$

    Find the value of y for $x = 3$ _____ and

                           $x = 9$ _____

  d. How is $y = \log_3(x)^2$ related to $y = \log_3(x)$?

  _____

  e. Graph $y = \log_3(x)^3$

    Find the value of y for $x = 3$ _____ and

                           $x = 9$ _____

  f. How is $y = \log_3(x)^3$ related to $y = \log_3(x)$?

  _____

  g. Will your conjecture be true for any a in $y = \log_3(x)^a$? Verify your answer by graphing the same equations with a different base. Show your results.

  _____

Computer Master 22

Solving $b^x = k$

Exponential equations can be solved graphically or algebraically. In each of the problems in this activity you are asked to use your computer grapher to approximate the solution to an equation and then to verify your work by solving the equation with logarithms. Round answers to the nearest tenth unless otherwise indicated.

1. Consider the equation $32 = 4^x$. Using your computer grapher, draw the graph of $y = 4^x$. Find the point on the graph that has 32 as its y-coordinate. What is the x-coordinate of that point? _____

2. To solve $32 = 4^x$ algebraically using common logarithms:

Take log of both sides of the equation:	$\log 32 = \log 4^x$
Use the Powering Property:	$\log 32 = x \log 4$
Solve for x:	$x = \dfrac{\log 32}{\log 4}$

   a. Using a calculator, find log 32 and log 4. Divide to find x. _____

   b. How does the answer compare to the answer you found graphically? _____

3. Use your computer grapher to approximate the solution to each equation. Then solve it algebraically using common logarithms. Compare the two solutions to each equation.

   a. $12^x = 0.5$ _____

   b. $1800 = 8.7^x$ _____

   c. $.087 = 3^{3x}$ _____

4. A *logarithmic spiral* based on the "golden ratio" can be produced using the equation:

$$y = \left(\frac{\sqrt{5} + 1}{2}\right)^e$$

where y is the distance from any point on the spiral to the pole of the spiral and x represents the rotation from a given base line.

   a. Graph the equation above. Then find the value of x for which the distance from the pole to the spiral is 3 units. Verify your answer algebraically. _____

Computer Master 22 (for use with Lesson 9-9)
Advanced Algebra © Scott, Foresman and Co.

Computer Master 22   (page 2)

b. In the same manner, find the value of x for
which the distance to the center is 0.28 units.   _____

c. If each unit of x represents 90° clockwise
rotation, then find the rotation to the nearest
degree for a point on the spiral 1.3 units from
the pole.   _____

5. Many prescribed drugs are used up by the human body at rates described
in terms of exponential decay. A patient suffering from bronchial asthma is
given 3 doses of 100 mg. of the drug theophylline every 4 hours to achieve
the desired therapeutic effect and regular maintenance dosages of 65 mg.
every 4 hours thereafter. The maintenance dosage, R is related to the half-
life of the drug (in hours), H by the formula:

$$R = 100(1 - e^{-8.3/H})$$

a. Graph the equation above on the interval $0 \leq$
$x \leq 100$ to approximate the half-life of the
drug to the nearest hour. Use 2.718 for e.   _____

b. Compute the half-life algebraically using
natural logarithms and compare the answers.   _____

Computer Master 23

Properties of Sines and Cosines

In BASIC the sine and cosine ratios can be found using the function abbreviations SIN and COS. However, since SIN(θ) and COS(θ) are computed from a unit called the radian, degrees must be converted to radians before either function is used. Radian is defined in Lesson 10-10. In the BASIC program below, SIN(D) and COS(D) are printed using the degree/radian conversion ratio of $\frac{\pi}{180} = 0.017453292$.

```
10  INPUT "ANGLE IN DEGREES"; D
20  PRINT "DEGREES", "SIN(D)", "COS(D)"
30  LET R = D * .017453292
40  PRINT D, SIN(R), COS(R)
50  END
```

1. a. RUN the program to print SIN 72° and COS 72°. _____

b. Evaluate sin 72° and cos 72° on your calculator. Which—your calculator or your program—gives more digits? _____

2. By the Exact Value Theorem, the sine and cosine ratios for certain angles have exact values.

a. RUN the program to approximate sin 30° and cos 30°. _____

b. What are the exact values of sin 30° and cos 30°? _____

c. Use the program to approximate the exact values for sin 45° and cos 45°. _____

d. What are the exact values of sin 45° and cos 45°? _____

e. Why aren't the exact values of sin θ or cos θ displayed on the computer or calculator? _____

3. a. Modify the program so as to use a FOR . . . NEXT loop to print a table of values of sin(D) and cos(D) for $0° \leq D \leq 90°$ in increments of 5°.

b. Based on your output, solve each equation.

sin 10° = cos D　　　　sin 55° = cos D　　　　cos 15° = sin D

$D =$ _____　　　$D =$ _____　　　$D =$ _____

c. What theorem do all values in the table verify? _____

Computer Master 23 (for use with Lesson 10-3)
Advanced Algebra © Scott, Foresman and Co.

Computer Master 23   (page 2)

4. a. Modify the FOR . . . NEXT loop so it prints a table of values for sin(D) and cos(D) for 0° ≤ D ≤ 360° in increments of 10°. Save a copy of your output.

b. What are the maximum and minimum values attained by sin(D)?   _____

c. What are the maximum and minimum values attained by cos(D)?   _____

d. If 90° < D < 180°, state the sign of each of sin(D) and cos(D).   _____

e. For what values of D is cos(D) negative?   _____

f. For what values of D are both cos(D) and sin(D) negative?   _____

g. Summarize in words the pattern of the signs of sin(D) and cos(D).

_____

5. Refer to the output you got for Question 4.

a. *True or false*   sin(D + 180°) = −sin(D)   _____

b. Find expressions identically equal to these expressions.

sin (D + 90°) = _____

cos(D + 90°) = _____

c. Find an equation other than those listed in Lesson 10-3 or on this Computer Master to describe a pattern in the table.   _____

6. a. Modify the original program as follows and run it.

```
20   PRINT "DEGREES", "SIN(D)", "COS(D)",
        "NEW FUNCTION"
40   PRINT D, SIN(R), COS(R), 2 * SIN(R) * COS(R)
```

b. Make a conjecture. For all D, 2 sin(D) cos(D) = _____

c. The formula in **b** above is sometimes called the Double-Angle formula for the Sine. Modify the program to determine which of the following is the Double-Angle formula for the Cosine:

$$\cos (2R) = 1 - 2(\cos(R))^2 \quad \text{or} \quad \cos(2R) = 1 - 2(\sin(R))^2$$

_____

Computer Master 24

The Sine and Cosine Functions

Trigonometric functions can be graphed using a computer grapher. Before you start, set your grapher so that it accepts x in degrees. Do the graphs for each problem on a separate pair of axes unless otherwise indicated.

1. Set the limits on the graph in the graphers to -360 to 540 on the x-axis and -5 to 5 on the y-axis. Draw the graph of $f(x) = \sin(x)$. Use the grapher to answer the following questions within the given domain:

   a. The function has six x-intercepts between -360 and 540. Name them.

   _____

   b. What is the maximum value of f over the interval from -360 to 540?   _____

   c. What is the minimum value of f?   _____

   d. Describe the range of the function.

   _____

   e. What are the x coordinates of the points in the interval for which $f(x)$ has its maximum value?   _____

   f. What is the next value of x beyond 540 at which $f(x)$ will have its maximum value?   _____

   g. Let n be any integer. Write an algebraic expression in terms of n to represent the x-coordinate of all points at which f has its maximum value.

   _____

2. Graph $f(x) = \cos(x)$. Use the grapher to answer the following:

   a. Name the x-intercepts between -360 and 540.   _____

   b. Describe the range of the cosine function.   _____

   c. Graph $f(x) = \sin(x)$ on the same graph. Find the coordinates of all points of intersection of the two functions between -360 and 540.

   _____

   d. Let n be any integer. Write an algebraic expression in terms of n to generate the x coordinate of all points of intersection of the two functions.

   _____

Computer Master 24   (page 2)

3. Set the limits on the graph in the grapher to -180 to 180 on the x-axis and -1 to 1 on the y-axis. Draw the graphs of $f(x) = \sin(x)$ and $f(x) = \cos(x)$. Use the grapher and its rescaling feature for the following:

a. Find sin 144° to the nearest tenth. Find another x such that $\sin(x) = \sin 144°$.   _____

b. Find two values of x such that $\cos(x) = \sin 144°$.   _____

c. Find sin $(-63°)$ to the nearest tenth. Find another x such that $\sin(x) = \sin(-63°)$.   _____

d. Find two values of x such that $\sin(x)$ is approximately .42.   _____

4. Graph $f(x) = \cos(x - 90)$.

5. This function is congruent to one of the sine or cosine functions. Which one?   _____

Find a value of n such that $\cos(x + n) = \cos(x)$. Verify your answer by graphing the functions $f(x) = \cos(x + n)$ and $g(x) = \cos(x)$ on the same axes.   _____

6. Draw the graph of $f(x) = \tan(x)$ between -180 and 180

a. The graph has three x-intercepts within the domain that is shown on the graph. What is the x coordinate of each?   _____

b. Does the function have a maximum or minimum value? If so, what are they?   _____

c. Use the rescaling feature to approximate the values of tan 18°, tan $(-75°)$, and tan 135° to the nearest tenth.   _____

d. Approximate tan 85°. Is it possible to approximate tan 90°? Explain.

_____

7. Experiment with various integral values of k (both positive and negative) to determine its effect on sine waves. Describe in words your conclusions:

a. $f(x) = k\sin(x)$ _____

b. $f(x) = \sin(kx)$ _____

c. $f(x) = \sin(x) + k$ _____

Computer Master 25
Radian Measure

Trigonometric functions in BASIC use the radian as the unit of measure for angles and rotations. Computer graphers usually allow the choice of either degrees or radians in graphing trigonometric functions.

1. RUN the BASIC program to calculate the radian equivalent of degrees:

```
10   LET PI = 3.141592654
20   PRINT "DEGREES", "RADIANS"
30   FOR D = 0 TO 180 STEP 10
40     LET R = PI * D / 180
50     PRINT D, R
60   NEXT D
70   END
```

Use the table to answer the following:

    a. Find 180 degrees in radians.   _____

    b. 40 degrees is about what fraction of a radian?   _____

    c. Find 2 radians to the nearest 10 degrees.   _____

    d. Find 1 radian to the nearest 10 degrees.   _____

2. Modify the loop in lines 30–60 so as to

    a. find the radian equivalent of each degree measure.

        61° _____   67° _____   74° _____

    b. find 1 radian to the nearest degree and also
        to a tenth of a degree.   _____

3. **a.** Make a graph of the relation between D and R.

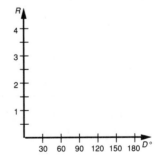

    b. Does the graph represent a linear function?

        _____

        If so, what is its slope?   _____

        What is its y-intercept?   _____

4. Now with your computer grapher, set the units to degrees and graph the cosine function from −540 to 360 degrees. Use the rescale feature of your grapher to answer the questions below.

    a. What is cos 25° to the nearest tenth?   _____

Computer Master 25 (for use with Lesson 10-10)
Advanced Algebra © Scott, Foresman and Co.

Computer Master 25   (page 2)

b. How many x-intercepts does the graph have on the domain $-540° \leq x \leq 360°$?

_____

Find them all.

_____

c. For how many values of x between $-540°$ and $360°$ is it true that $\cos x = 1$?

_____

Find those values.

_____

d. For how many x-values between $0°$ and $360°$ is it true that $\cos x = .2$?

_____

Approximate these x-values to the nearest degree.

_____

5. a. Choose degrees as the unit of measure, and with the limits for the graph set from -180 to 180 on the x-axis and from -1 to 1 on the y-axis, draw the graph of $y = \sin(x)$.

b. Change the unit of measurement to radians. What limits must be set on the x-axis to draw the same graph as in part **a**? Graph $y = \sin(x)$ to verify your answer.

_____

6. Use your graph from Question 5, and the zoom, rescale or scroll features, if necessary, to do the following:

a. Approximate $\sin 1.57$ to the nearest tenth.

_____

b. Approximate $\sin \dfrac{\pi}{5}$ to the nearest tenth.

_____

c. Find two values of x to the nearest tenth of a radian such that $\sin(x) = .5$.

_____

d. Find two values of x to the nearest tenth of a radian such that $\sin(x) = -1$.

_____

e. According to the graph, for how many real numbers x, where $-\pi \leq x \leq \pi$, is it true that $\sin(x) = .85$?

_____

Find all such x to the nearest tenth.

_____

Computer Master 26

The Factor Theorem

The x-intercepts of the graph of a polynomial function are called the zeroes of the function since the value of the polynomial at each x-intercept is 0. Use the computer grapher to do each problem on a separate pair of axes.

1. Graph $f(x) = (x - 8)(x + 2)(5x - 3)$.

   a. At how many points does the graph intersect
   the x-axis?   _____

   b. How many zeroes does the function have?   _____

   c. Use the function grapher to determine the
   coordinates of each x-intercept.   _____

   d. What are the zeroes of the function?   _____

2. Set the limits on the window of the function grapher from -100 to 100 on the y-axis and from -10 to 10 on the x-axis.

   a. Graph $f(x) = (x - 1)(4 - x)(2x + 7)$.
   Find the zeroes of the function.   _____

   b. On the same set of axes graph $y =$
   $(x - 1)(x - 4)(2x + 7)$. What are its
   zeroes?   _____

   c. Compare and contrast the two graphs.

   _____

3. The zeroes of a polynomial function are $-6, 3,$ and 5.

   a. Find such a function and draw its graph.

   b. Find another polynomial with the same zeroes and draw its graph.

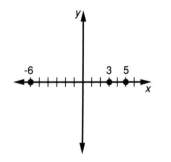

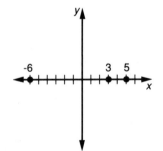

function: $y =$ _____   function: $y =$ _____

Computer Master 26 (for use with Lesson 11-4)
Advanced Algebra © Scott, Foresman and Co.

Computer Master 26 (page 2)

4. A polynomial function has zeroes at -2, 1.5, and 4.25. Find an equation and sketch a graph for such a function that is

a. cubic   **b.** 4th degree   **c.** 5th degree

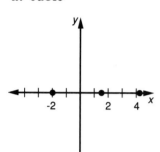 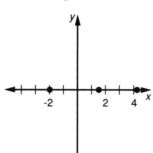 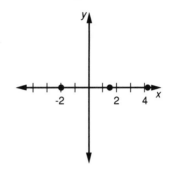

$y =$ _____ $y =$ _____ $y =$ _____

In 5–7, **a.** graph the function; **b.** identify its zeroes; **c.** rewrite the polynomial as a product of linear factors.

5. $y = x^3 + 3x^2 - 22x - 24$ _____   _____

6. $y = -2x^3 - x^2 + 52x - 84$ _____   _____

7. $y = 4x^4 - 45x^2 + 20x + 21$ _____   _____

8. Set the limits on the window of the function grapher from -5 to 5 on the x-axis and -10 to 10 on the y-axis.

    a. Graph $f(x) = x - 3$. On the same axes graph $f(x) = (x - 3)^2$, $f(x) = (x - 3)^3$, and $f(x) = (x - 3)^4$.

    b. What is the zero of each function?   _____

    c. What would you expect to be the shape of
       $f(x) = (x - 3)^5$?   _____

    d. Describe in words or sketch what you think the graphs of $y = x + 4$, $y = (x + 4)^2$, $y = (x + 4)^3$, and $y = (x + 4)^4$ would look like. (After you have written your conjecture, clear the screen with the graphs of parts **a-c,** and draw these graphs.)

    _____

    e. Make a hypothesis about the shape of any graph $f(x) = (x - a)^n$.

    _____

Computer Master 27

Estimating Zeroes

Estimation of zeroes without a computer is a difficult process. However, a computer grapher or a relatively simple BASIC program allows you to do very accurate approximations quite simply. In this activity you will use each to determine the zeroes of a polynomial.

1. Set the limits on the graph in the computer grapher from -5 to 5 on the x-axis and -10 to 10 on the y-axis. Draw the graph of $f(x) = x^3 + 2x^2 - 5x - 3$.

   a. How many zeroes does the function have?   _____

   b. How many zeroes have positive values?   _____

   c. Between what pair of consecutive integers is the value of each zero?   _____

2. On the same graph, use the rescale feature of the grapher to do the following:

   a. Approximate the largest zero to the nearest tenth.   _____

   b. Approximate the largest zero to the nearest hundredth.   _____

   c. Approximate the value of each of the other two zeroes to the nearest tenth.   _____

3. The following BASIC program can be used to print a table values for a function $f(x)$ from $x = A$ to $x = B$ in increments of C.

```
 10   REM PROGRAM TO PRINT TABLE OF
          FUNCTIONAL VALUES
 20   INPUT "ENDPOINTS A AND B OF DOMAIN"; A, B
 30   INPUT "STEP SIZE"; C
 40   DEF FN F(X) = _____
 50   PRINT "X", "F(X)"
 60   FOR X = A TO B STEP C
 70     PRINT X, FN F(X)
 80   NEXT X
 90   INPUT "TRY AGAIN? (Y/N)"; A$
100   IF A$ = "Y" THEN 10
110   END
```

   a. Enter the function $f(x) = 2x^3 + 15x^2 + 32x + 16$ on line 40 and RUN the program using -5 and 5 for A and B respectively, and 1 for the step size.

Computer Master 27 (for use with Lesson 11-5)
Advanced Algebra © **Scott**, Foresman and Co.

b. Is there an integer value of x for which $f(x)$
= 0? If so, what integer is a zero of the
function?   _____

c. One way to locate non-integral zeroes is to look for opposite signs in
pairs of consecutive values for $f(x)$. One zero lies between -3 and -2.
RUN the program using -3 and -2 for A and B respectively. What is
the value of this zero

to the nearest integer?   _____

to the nearest tenth?   _____

to the nearest hundredth?   _____

d. Approximate the other zero to the nearest
hundredth.   _____

4. The polynomial function $f(x) = 3x^4 + 25x^3 - 53x^2 - 54x + 72$ has
4 zeroes between -10 and 10. Use either a computer grapher or a
BASIC program to find each zero to the nearest
tenth.   _____

5. Beginning in January 1985, and each year thereafter, Mr. Ramirez deposits
$2000 in an IRA (Individual Retirement Account) which compounds
interest at rate r annually. Assume no additional money is deposited and
no money is withdrawn.

a. Write a polynomial in x where $x = 1 + r$
that represents the amount in the account in
early February 1993.   _____

b. If the bank pays 6% interest during the entire
period, calculate the amount in the IRA in
February 1993.   _____

c. At what rate (to the nearest tenth) would Mr.
Ramirez have to invest in order to have at
least $30,000 in the account?   _____

Computer Master 28

Classifying Conics

In order to do this activity, your computer grapher must be able to graph
quadratic equations in general form: $Ax^2 + Bxy + Cy^2 + Dx + Ey + F = 0$. Do each problem on a separate pair of axes.

1. Graph and identify the conic section for each equation:

a. $3x^2 + 4xy + 2y^2 + 5x - 3y + 4 = 0$ _____

b. $-4x^2 + 6xy + y - 5 = 0$ _____

c. $2x^2 - y + 8 = 0$ _____

d. $4x^2 + 9y^2 = 36$ _____

e. $6y + 4 + 2x = 3y^2$ _____

2. Use each set of values in the general form of a quadratic equation to draw
a graph. Then compute B^2 and $4AC$:

	A	B	C	D	E	F	Name	B^2	$4AC$
a.	4	4	1	8	-6	5	_____	___	___
b.	-4	8	-5	9	-15	30	_____	___	___
c.	3	-9	0	2	-3	-15	_____	___	___
d.	-2	-7	-5	0	0	8	_____	___	___
e.	0	0	-4	3	-4	6	_____	___	___
f.	3	0	2	-9	18	-45	_____	___	___

3. From the table in problem 2, compare ($>$, $=$, $<$) the values of B^2 and
$4AC$ for each of the three different conic sections.

_____

4. For each set of values, determine what values of C can be used in the
quadratic equation to make its graph a parabola, an hyperbola, and an
ellipse. Draw the graphs to check your work.

a. $A = 8, B = 8, D = 1, E = -8, F = -7$ _____

b. $A = -3, B = 9, D = -9, E = 2, F = 8$ _____

Computer Master 28 (for use with Lesson 12-8)
Advanced Algebra © Scott, Foresman and Co.

Computer Master 28   (page 2)

5. For what value of k will the equation
$-x^2 + 6xy + x = 6 + ky^2$ be a parabola?
Graph the equation to verify your answer.   _____

6. Can a quadratic equation in which $A = 4$, $C = -6$, $D = 0$, $E = 0$, and
$F = 12$ be any of the three conic sections depending on the value of B?
Specify which conics and what values of B.

_____

7. Without drawing its graph, predict whether $-8x^2 - 7xy + 6y^2 = 0$ will
be an ellipse, parabola, or hyperbola. Then graph the equation. Explain
why the result is consistent or inconsistent with your previous work in this
activity.

_____

Computer Master 29

Quadratic Systems

In solving the systems of equations in this activity, you can use your computer grapher to graph quadratic equations either in their general form or by first solving for y in terms of x, using the form:

$$y = \frac{-(Bx + E) \pm \sqrt{(Bx + E) - 4(C)(Ax + Dx + F)}}{2C}$$

1. In a free market, the price of a bushel of wheat is determined by the size of the wheat harvest and consumer demand for wheat. Suppose the demand for wheat is modeled by the equation $xy = 7$ and the supply of wheat by $4y - x^2 - 1 = 0$ where x is the monthly harvest of wheat in millions of bushels, and y is the price of a bushel of wheat. Set the limits on your grapher from 0 to 10 along each axis and graph the two equations on the same axes. Then using the graph:

   a. Estimate the price to the nearest cent that a farmer can expect to receive for one bushel of wheat. _____

   b. Estimate, to the nearest hundredth, the millions of bushels of wheat that will be sold at that price. _____

   c. Calculate the revenues in millions of dollars that can be expected from all wheat sales. _____

To do problem 2, use the same set of axes you used to do problem 1. *Do not* clear the graphs from problem 1.

2. Because of a large harvest, the amount of wheat that farmers are willing to sell at any given price increases so that the supply can be modeled by the equation $5y - 2x^2 - 2 = 0$. Graph this equation. Then using this graph along with the graphs from problem 1:

   a. Estimate the price to the nearest cent that a farmer can now expect to receive for one bushel of wheat. _____

   b. Calculate the revenues that can be expected from wheat sales at the new price and compare it with the expected revenue at the price computed in problem 1.

   _____

   c. The demand curve in this problem has an *elasticity* of 1. What do you think that means?

   _____

Computer Master 29   (page 2)

d. Suppose demand is modeled by $xy + x = 9$ instead of $xy = 7$. Using the same two equations for the old and new supply curves, graph all three equations on the same axes. Use calculations to explain whether or not the new demand curve has an elasticity of 1.

---

3. Square County has weather stations at A and B as shown:

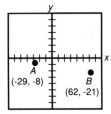

a. Graph two circles with radii 65, one with its center at A and the other with its center at B. Approximate the coordinates of the two points at which the circles intersect. (Round to whole numbers.)

b. The line connecting the intersections divides the county into two regions. Which region appears to have the greater area?

c. Explain how the size and shape of the regions would change if a radius other than 65 were used.

---

d. Describe a fair way to compute an average daily temperature for the county using the temperature readings at A and B.

---

4. The county builds a third weather station C at (48, 91).

a. Graph three circles each with radius 65 at A, B, and C. Approximate the coordinates of the points at which the circles intersect. (Round to whole numbers.)

b. Do you think a radius other than 65 could be used in locating the intersections? Explain why or why not.

---

c. Make a sketch showing the best way to divide the county into three weather regions.

Computer Master 30

Using BASIC with Series

The following BASIC program can be used to compute the sum of any arithmetic series recursively where N is the number of terms, AN is the nth term of the sequence, D is the common difference between terms, and SUM is the sum of the first N terms of the sequence.

```
10  REM PROGRAM TO PRINT TERMS OF
        ARITHMETIC SEQUENCE AND SUM OF SERIES
15  INPUT "FIRST TERM"; AN
20  INPUT "COMMON DIFFERENCE"; D
30  LET SUM = AN
35  PRINT "N", "TERM", "SUM"
40  FOR K = 1 TO N
45    PRINT K, AN, SUM
50    AN = AN + D
55    SUM = SUM + AN
60  NEXT K
65  END
```

In 1 and 2, (a) RUN the program, and list the last line of the output for each of the following sequences; (b) Check your work by calculating the values of a_n and S_n using explicit formulas.

1. Five terms; the first term is 7; the common difference is 25

   a) _____

   b) _____

2. Fifteen terms; the first term is 21; each term is 12 less than the previous one.

   a) _____

   b) _____

In 3–6, use the program to compute the sum of each series.

3. $5 + 14 + 23 + 32 + 41 + 50 + 59$ _____

4. $1 + 2 + 3 + 4 + \ldots + 48$ _____

5. The first 20 multiples of 7   _____

6. The sum of the first 12 terms in: $-17, -12.5,$
   $-8, -3.5, \ldots$ _____

In 7 and 8, consider that when a parachutist jumps from an airplane, the distances in feet fallen in successive seconds before pulling the rip cord form an arithmetic sequence 16, 48, 80, ... Use the program to find:

7. a. the distance fallen during the 7th second.   _____

   b. the distance covered in a 7-second free-fall.   _____

Computer Master 30 (for use with Lessons 13-1, 13-2, and 13-4)
Advanced Algebra © Scott, Foresman and Co.

8. the free-fall time to the nearest second of a
jump from a plane at 4,000 feet, if the rip cord
must be pulled at 1,000 feet above the ground.   _____

**In 9 and 10, modify the program to compute terms of a geometric sequence
and its series from three inputs N, AN, and R, the constant ratio. RUN the
program and list the last line of the output for the geometric sequence
described below:**

9. six terms; the first term is 5; the constant ratio is
3   _____

10. eleven terms beginning with $24, 12, 6, 3, \frac{3}{2}, \ldots$ _____

11. a. Use the program as modified for Questions 9 and 10 to print a table
with the first 12 terms of the geometric sequence $1, -4, 16, -64, \ldots$,
and the sum $S = 1 - 4 + 16 - 64 + \ldots$,
as n goes from 1 to 12. Record the last line of
output.   _____

    b. Show how to calculate the values reported in part **a** using explicit
formulas.

_____

12. Let S_n be the sum of the first n terms of the infinite geometric series
$100 + 90 + 81 + \ldots$

    a. Use the program in Questions 9 and 10 to
find S_{15}.   _____

    b. Find S_{25}.   _____

    c. Find a value of n such that $S_n > 950$.   _____

    d. Does S_n ever exceed 1000? If so, for what value of n is $S_n > 1000$? If
not, what is the largest value S_n can have?

_____

**In 13, note that a chain letter is intended to create a geometric sequence.
Recipients of a letter receive a list of names and are instructed to remove the
top name, add their name to the list, then send a specified number of copies
to other people. Use your BASIC program from Questions 9 and 10 to
answer the following:**

13. Amy Xerox receives a letter with a list of 5 names that requests each
recipient to make and send 4 copies to friends. If no one breaks the chain,
how many letters will be mailed containing
Amy's name somewhere in the list?   _____

ANSWER KEY

Computer Master 1

1. a. 5, 9, 13, 17, 21, 25
   b. explicit
   c. 10   FOR N = 1 TO 20

2. 0, 1.5, 3, 4.5, 6, 7.5

3. 10   FOR N = 1 TO 12
   20   LET T = $2 \wedge$ N; 4096

4. a. recursive
   b. 5, 9, 13, 17, 21, 25, 29, 33, 37, 41
   c. 10   LET T = 86
   40   LET T = T − 11
   d. 10   LET T = 9
   40   LET T = 5 * T

5. 1, 1, R + S, S, T
   a. 1, 1, 2, 3, 5, 8, 13, 21, 34, 55
   b. 50   FOR N = 3 TO 22
   c. S/R is the golden ratio, 1.618

Computer Master 2

1. a. direct
   b. inverse
   c. $y = \dfrac{x}{4}$ is a straight line with a slope of $\dfrac{1}{4}$; as x gets larger, y gets larger. $y = \dfrac{4}{x}$ is an hyperbola in Quadrants I and III; as x gets larger positive, y gets smaller, and as x gets larger negative, y gets smaller

2. b. Sample: $y = 3x^2$, $y = -3x^2$, $y = 4x^3$, $y = -4x^3$
   c. $y = 3x^2$ direct when $x > 0$, inverse when $x < 0$; $y = -3x^2$ direct when $x < 0$, inverse when $x > 0$; $y = 4x^2$ direct; $y = -4x^2$ inverse

3. a. Both graphs are hyperbolas, and both inverse variations.
   b. For all real numbers x, $x = 0$, the range of $y = \dfrac{1}{x}$ is all real numbers y, $y = 0$; the range of $y = \dfrac{1}{x^2}$ is $y > 0$.
   c. $0 < x < 1$
   d. $x > 1$

4. a. $\dfrac{1}{x^3}$ will look similar to $\dfrac{1}{x}$, but with a steeper curve.

Computer Master 3

1. The three lines are parallel. The fourth line is parallel to the three lines.

2. The lines have the same y-intercept.

3. As m, in the general equation $y = mx + b$, gets larger the graph gets steeper.

4. $y = 4x - 5$

5. a. $y = 7$
   b. $y = -13$
   c. $x = 2$
   d. $y = 13$
   e. $x = 2.4$

6. a. 59°F
   b. −5°C
   c. 22°C
   d. 10.4°F

Computer Master 4

1. a. 10; 10 − 31
   b. 40   IF N = 15 THEN 70

2. 20   LET T = 7 + 9 * (N − 1)
   40   IF N = 15 THEN 70

3. 20   LET T = 4 − 12 * (N − 1)
   40   IF N = 20 THEN 70

4. 20   LET T = −33 + 5 * (N − 1)
   40   IF N = 12 THEN 70

5. a. 10   LET N = 3
   20   LET S = 180 * (N − 2)
   30   PRINT N, S
   b. 10

6. 20   LET T = 7 + 12 * (N − 2)
   30   IF T > = 200 THEN 70
   40   PRINT N, T

7. 29

---

5. a. The shape of the curve becomes more rounded.
   b. The shape of the curve becomes more rounded as k increases.

6. asymptote: $y = -1$;
   axis of symmetry: $x = 0$

7. asymptote: $y = 0$;
   axis of symmetry: $x = 1$

8. asymptote: $y = 0$;
   axis of symmetry: $x = -2$

9. asymptote: $y = 2$;
   axis of symmetry: $x = 0$

---

8. 15   LET T = 16
   20   PRINT N, T
   30   LET T = T − 9
   40   IF N = 10 THEN 70

9. a. no; the difference between the values of each term and that of the preceding term increases for each term.
   b. The sequence of the differences between each successive pair of terms is arithmetic.
   c. T = 1; R = 3

Computer Master 5

1. a. Yes
   b. No
   c. No

2. a. Yes
   b. Yes
   c. No

3. a. $y \le x - 2$
   b. $y < -3x + 7$

4. Sample: $y > x - 3$; $y < x + 3$; $y > -x - 3$; $y < -x + 3$

5. a. about −4.5
   b. $x \le -4\dfrac{1}{2}$
   c. $x > -4\dfrac{1}{2}$

6. $x < -2$

7. a. The point on the graph (1.25, 3.25) is not in the solution set.
   b. 1.1 million
   c. $y \ge 4.0 - 2.5x$; .3 million

Computer Master Answers
Advanced Algebra © Scott, Foresman and Co.

Computer Master 6

1. a. $y = -\frac{1}{2}x + 3$

  b. They are negative reciprocals of one another. Their product is -1.

2. a. $-\frac{2}{3}$

  b. $\frac{3}{2}$

  c. answers will vary; e.g. $y = \frac{3}{2}x$

  d. $y = \frac{3}{2}x + k$; k will vary

  e. $y = \frac{3}{2}x + k$

3. a. $y = \frac{1}{5}x + 1$

4. a. $y = -\frac{4}{3}x$

  b. $y = \frac{3}{4}x$

5. b. $y = 3x + 9$

6. True

7. $y = -2x + 12, y = -2x,$
$y = \frac{1}{2}x - \frac{1}{2}, y = \frac{1}{2}x + 7$

8. answers will vary

9. b. $(1, 1), (-6, -6), (-1, 9)$

  c. $y = -\frac{1}{3}x + \frac{4}{3}$

Computer Master 7

1. $(0, -5)$

2. $(-1, 2)$

3. $\{(-4, 3), (6, -2)\}$

4. $(-1.5, -8.5)$

5. $(2.0, -3.4), (-2.0, -3.4)$

6. $(-24, -129)$

7. inconsistent

8. $2.67; 2.34$ tons

9. a. $6x + 4y = 180$
    $xy = 150$

  b. $(26.2, 5.7)$ and $(3.9, 38.4)$

  c. 26.2 ft wide and 5.7 ft long; 3.9 ft wide and 38.4 ft long

Computer Master 8

1. a. The total number of computers cannot exceed 60.

  b. The total cost of the computers cannot exceed \$36,000.

  c. 1200, 1800, 960; 1200, 960; 1200

  d. 48 Peach; 0 Little Red

2. a. $(0, 60), (30, 30), (48, 0)$

  b. 1230; it intersects the feasible region at a vertex and exceeds all other values of u that intersect at vertices.

  c. 30 Peach; 30 Little Red

3. a. $(0, 50), (15, 35), (36, 0)$

  b. 15 Peach; 35 Little Red; 935 hours (answers may vary slightly above or below 935)

4. 36 Peach; 0 Little Red

5. If the ratio of the price of the more expensive computer to the price of the less expensive one is less than the usage ratio for the two computers, then only the more expensive computer will be used.

Computer Master 9

1. a. $h = -16t^2 + 80t$

  c. 60-65 ft

  d. 64 ft

  e. 1.4, 3.6

  f. 2.5

  g. 100 ft

  h. 5

2. a. $h = -16t^2 + 40t$

  b. Yes

  c. No; The second goes $\frac{1}{4}$ as high as the first.

3. a. $h = -4.9t^2 + 36t + 8800$

  c. 8852 m; 8852.4 m

  d. 8866 m

  e. 3.7

  f. 7.4 sec; 46 sec

4. $h = -16t^2 + 48t + 14; 48$ ft/sec

5. $h = -16t^2 + 64t; 64$ ft/sec or $h = -4.9t^2 + 19.6t; 19.6$ m/sec

Computer Master 10

1. a. $x = 0; (0, 0)$
    $x = 3; (3, 0)$
    $x = 0; (0, 7)$
    $x = 3; (3, 7)$

  b. $(1, 7)$

  c. $h; k; x = h; (h, k)$

2. a. $x = 0; (0, 0)$
    $x = -5; (-5, 0)$
    $x = 0; (0, 1)$
    $x = -5; (-5, 1)$

  b. It is the image of the graph of $y = -2x^2$ under the translation 5 units to the left and 4 units down.

3. a. $x = h; (h, k)$

  b. $a > 0; a < 0$

  c. $y = ax^2$

4. b. $y = .2(x + 1)^2 - 3$ or $y + 3 = .2(x + 1)^2$

5. $y = 5(x + 2)^2 + 4$ or $y = -5(x + 2)^2 + 4$

6. $y = -\frac{1}{2}(x - 8)^2 + 3$

7. $y = 3x^2 + 12x + 16$

8. b. $(-6, 2)$

  c. $h = -6; k = 2$

9. c. $x = 0$ and $y = 7$

  d. Yes; $T_{0,7}$

10. b. $y = \frac{-12}{(x - 2)} - 3$

11. a. $y = \frac{8}{(x + 5)^2} - 3$

Computer Master 11

1. a. 2

  b. two

  c. $(2, 0)$ and $(-5, 0)$

  d. 2 and -5

2. a. None

  b. 1.4 and 6.6

  c. -7

3. overshoot; the projectile hits the ground 28,500 ft from the cannon. A half-mile is 2640 ft.

4. a. None

  b. -8; less than 0

  c. two

  d. 136; greater than 0

  e. $c = 8$

  f. All three graphs have the same axis of symmetry.

  g. Many answers are possible. Students should find that the axis of symmetry is $x = 2$.

5. a. two

  b. make $b = 12$;
    $y = 2x^2 + 12x + 18$

  c. No, the parabolas have different axes of symmetry.

  d. $x = \frac{-b}{2(2)} = \frac{-b}{4}$

  e. $x = \frac{-b}{2a}$

Computer Master 12

1. a. SQR(x) = The positive square root of a non-negative number x.
   b. ABS(x) = The absolute value of any number x.
   c. If x > 0, SGN(x) = 1; if x = 0, SGN(x) = 0; if x < 0, SGN(x) = −1.

2. a.
   1   3
   2   6
   3   9
   4   12
   5   15
   6   18
   b. A table of values for the function, f(x) = 3x, is produced for integer values of x from 1 to 6.

3. a. square numbers:
   10   DEF FN F(X) = X∧2
   20   FOR X = 0 TO 10

   the powers of 2:
   10   DEF FN F(X) = 2∧X
   20   FOR X = 0 TO 10
   b. D = {0, 1, 5, 6, 7, 8, 9, 10}
   D = {2, 4}
   D = {3}

4. a. 10   DEF FN F(X) = 4*X∧2 − 9*X + 3
   b. −2; x = 2; f(−5)
   c. parabola

5. a. yes; x = 8
   b. x = −1.5

6. a.
   0   −8
   1   −3
   2   2
   3   7
   4   12
   5   17
   6   22
   b.
   0   −8
   1   2
   2   12
   3   22
   4   32
   5   42
   6   52
   no; the difference increases by multiples of 5 for each successive term.
   c. 30   PRINT X, FN (X + 4)

Computer Master 13

1. a. They are intersecting lines.
   b. They are parallel lines.

2. They are parallel lines, each with a slope of −6.

3. a. f(x) is an hyperbola; g(x) is a line. The domain of f(x) is restricted to x ≠ 0.
   b. f(x) and f(g(x)) are both hyperbolas. g(x) is a line.
   c. Both are hyperbolas. The asymptotes are x = −3 and y = 0 for f(g(x)) and x = 0 and y = 3 for g(f(x)).
   d. f(g(x)): x ≠ 3; g(f(x)): x ≠ 0

4. a. f(x) is a parabola; g(x) is a line. f(g(x)) and g(f(x)) are both parabolas.
   b. f(x) is an hyperbola; g(x) is a parabola. f(g(x)) and g(f(x)) are both inverse square curves.
   c. f(x) is an hyperbola; g(x) is an hyperbola. f(g(x)) and g(f(x)) are both lines with reciprocal slopes.
   d. f(x) is an inverse square; g(x) is a parabola. f(g(x)) and g(f(x)) are both inverse square curves.

5.
Line   Parabola Hyperbola   Inverse Square
Parabola Parabola Inverse Square Inverse Square
Hyperbola Inverse Square Line   Parabola
Inverse Square Inverse Square Parabola Parabola

6. Although f(g(x)) and g(f(x)) produce the same type of curve in each case, the two curves are not congruent.

7. The two graphs are both inverse squares.

Computer Master 14

1. a. C = 1.49 + .42*W
   b. $2.71
   c. 20   FOR W = .5 TO 10 STEP .5
   d. 6 lbs.

2. a. FN F(X) rounds X to the nearest ten.
   b. FN F(X) rounds X to the nearest hundred.
   c. 30   DEF FN F(X) = 1000 * INT((X + 500) / 1000)

3. a. 10   INPUT "ENTER SCORE"; X
   30   DEF FN F(X) = 4 − INT((100 − X) / 7)
   40   PRINT "GRADE ="; FN F(X)
   b. A   94 - 100
   B   87 - 93
   C   80 - 86
   D   73 - 79
   F   below 73
   c. example:
   DEF FN F(X) = 4 − INT((100 − X) / 10)
   A   91 - 100
   B   81 - 90
   C   71 - 80
   D   61 - 70
   F   below 61

4. a. 10   INPUT "ENTER TAXABLE INCOME"; X
   20   DEF FN F(X) = 7753 − (14 * INT((35999 − X) / 50))
   30   PRINT "YOUR TAX IS"; FN F(X)
   b. See table below. Change the following lines in the program:
   10   PRINT "AT LEAST   BUT NOT MORE   THAN   TAX"
   30   FOR X = 36000 TO 36950 STEP 50
   40   PRINT X, X + 50, FN F(X)
   50   NEXT X
   c. 20   DEF FN F(X) = 6206 − (14 * INT((35999 − X) / 50))

36,000	36,050	7,767	6,220	8.157	6,980
36,050	36,100	7,781	6,234	8.174	6,994
36,100	36,150	7,795	6,248	8.190	7,008
36,150	36,200	7,809	6,262	8.207	7,022
36,200	36,250	7,823	6,276	8.223	7,036
36,250	36,300	7,837	6,290	8.240	7,050
36,300	36,350	7,851	6,304	8.256	7,064
36,350	36,400	7,865	6,318	8.273	7,078
36,400	36,450	7,879	6,332	8.289	7,092
36,450	36,500	7,893	6,346	8.306	7,106
36,500	36,550	7,907	6,360	8.322	7,120
36,550	36,600	7,921	6,374	8.339	7,134
36,600	36,650	7,935	6,388	8.355	7,148
36,650	36,700	7,949	6,402	8.372	7,162
36,700	36,750	7,963	6,416	8.388	7,176
36,750	36,800	7,977	6,430	8.405	7,190
36,800	36,850	7,991	6,444	8.421	7,204
36,850	36,900	8,005	6,458	8.438	7,218
36,900	36,950	8,019	6,472	8.454	7,232
36,950	37,000	8,033	6,486	8.471	7,246

Computer Master 15

1. a. $h = 0; k = -2$
b. $h = -5; k = 0$

2. a. $y = |x + 1| + 2$
b. $y = |x - 4| - 2$

3. a. $|a|$ determines the slope. If $x > 0$, the slope is $|a|$. If $x < 0$, the slope is $-|a|$.
b. If $a > 0$, then the graphs of $y = a|x|$ and $y = |ax|$ are congruent. If $a < 0$, then $y = a|x|$ is the reflection image of $y = |ax|$ over the x-axis.

4. a. $y = -|x| + 2$
b. $y = 5|x + 3|$

5. The magnitude of a determines the "steepness." As $|a|$ increases the graph increases more rapidly. If $a > 0$, $y = ax$ is in the 1st and 3rd quadrants. If $a < 0$, $y = ax$ is in the 2nd and 4th quadrants.

6. a. $g(x) = (x - 3)^4$
b. $g(x) = (x + 2)^5 - 1$
c. true

7. a. $y = 4(x - 4)^2 + 1$
b. $y = (x - 4)^4 + 1$
c. The graphs are not congruent. Between $x = 4$ and $x = 5$ the quadratic rises more quickly.

8. a. $0 < x < 1; x = 0, x = 1; x > 1$
b. $x = -7, x = -2$
c. $x = \{-3, 3\}$

Computer Master 16

1. Because each is the image of the other reflected across $y = x$, they are inverses.

2. a. no
b. yes
c. no
d. yes

3. $y = \frac{1}{3}x + 2$

4. The equation of the line is $y = -\frac{1}{4}x + 5$. Its inverse is $y = -4x + 20$

5. $y = \frac{3 - x}{x}$

6. a. If a horizontal line can be drawn to intersect f(x) at more than one point, then the inverse of f(x) is not a function..
b. Either $x \geq 0$ or $x \leq 0$
c. $y = \frac{\sqrt{2x}}{2}$

7. a. $x \geq 5; f^{-1}(x) = \sqrt{x} + 5$
b. Either $x > 0$ or $x < 0$; $y = \frac{\sqrt{x}}{2x}$

Computer Master 17

1. a. recursive
b.

YEAR	AMOUNT
1	5350.00
2	5724.50
3	6125.22
4	6553.98
5	7012.76
6	7503.65
7	8028.91
8	8590.93
9	9192.30
10	9835.76

c. $350
d. $643.46
e. $4835.76
f. 6 years
g. 16 years

2.

```
 5   PRINT "CURRENT
        TUITION, AVG.
        INTEREST, NO. OF
        YEARS";
15   PRINT "YEAR", "TUITION"
```

1	8800.00
2	9680.00
3	10648.00
4	11712.80
5	12884.08
6	14172.49
7	15589.74
8	17148.71
9	18863.58
10	20749.94
11	22824.94
12	25107.53
13	27618.18
14	30379.99
15	33417.99
16	36759.79
17	40435.77
18	44479.35

3. a. 9 years
b. 12 years
c. 18 years
d. The annual rate times the approximate number of years to double the investment is always equal to 72.
e. 2% takes about 36 years to double.
12% takes about 6 years to double.

4. a. $1181.02
b. $11194.05
c. $1195.62
d. $1196.68
e. $1197.19
f. $6.17

Computer Master 18 (right column)

5. a. Investing for one year at 7% compounded annually is a better deal.
$1000 invested at 7% compounded annually after 1 year = $1070.00
$1000 invested at 6% compounded monthly after 1 year = $1061.68
b. 7% compounded annually is still a better deal.
$1000 invested at 7% compounded annually after 5 years = $1402.55
$1000 invested at 6% compounded monthly after 5 years = $1348.85

Computer Master 18

1. a. 10   1310720
b. 20   LET T = $3 * 4 \wedge (N - 1)$

2. 10   FOR N = 1 TO 12
20   LET T = $16 * 2 \wedge (N - 1)$

3. 10   FOR N = 1 TO 25
20   LET T = $200 * .1 \wedge (N - 1)$

4. 10   FOR N = 1 TO 15
20   LET T = $-7 * 3 \wedge (N - 1)$

5. b. 2
c. 2
d. 2
e. 2

6. a. Brazil; 183,100,000; US: 267,600,000
b. about 35 years; 314,200,000
c. In about 2030 the population of Brazil will be about 331,700,000 and that of the US will be about 329,900,000.

7. a. 1.3 is a reasonable estimate
b. 83.2; 308.9
c. 191.1 is the estimate using 1.2 instead of 1.3. It's about one third of the estimate in part **b.**

Computer Master Answers
Advanced Algebra © Scott, Foresman and Co.

73

Computer Master 19

1. It intersects the y-axis at $+5$. It doesn't intersect the x-axis since 2 is positive for all x.

2. a. $y = 20$
b. $y = 5$
c. $y = 2.5$
d. $x = 3.3$
e. $y = 34.8$

3. a. $(0, 1)$
b. As b increases, the graph increases more steeply. The graph passes through $(0, 1)$. All have shape:

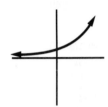

c. The graph passes through $(0, 1)$. As x increases, y approaches the x-axis. As b approaches 0, the graph decreases more rapidly. The graph is shaped like:

4. a. $|a|$ determines the steepness of the curve.
b. If $a > 0$, the curve turns up as x increases; if $a < 0$, the curve turns down as x increases.

5. $x = 4.18$

6. a. $(1, 24)$
b. Sample: $y = 2 \cdot 5^x$ and $y = 5 \cdot 2^x$; $(1, 10)$
c. The graphs intersect at $(1, ab)$

7. a. 387.0
b. The actual CPI was 330.5 which is less than 387.0 so the inflation rate was less.
c. 6.0%

Computer Master 20

1. a. 0; 1; 0 and 1; -2 and -1
b. .7 and .8
c. .77 and .78; .8
d. .78
e. 2.2
f. $-.3$
g. 1.4

2. a. 6
b. 3.83
c. -4.6
d. $n = 8.8$

3. a. 2.8
b. $-.8$
c. $n = -1$
d. $n = -.6$
e. -2.5
f. $x = .2$

Computer Master 21

1. a. $x = 10^y$
b. $y = 10^x$

2. a. 0
b. .5
c. 3.2
d. $\log (3.2) = .5$ because $10^{0.5} = 3.2$

3. a. 1
b. 1
c. 1
d. 1
e. $y = \log_b (x)$ will always have an x-intercept of 1 because $b^0 = 1$ for any b.

4. b. $y = 1; y = 2$
c. $y = 2; y = 4$
d. $\log_3 (x)^2 = 2 \cdot \log_3 (x)$
e. $y = 3; y = 6$
f. $\log_3 (x)^3 = 3 \cdot \log_3 (x)$
g. yes

Computer Master 22

1. 2.5

2. a. about 2.5
b. The same

3. a. $x \approx -.3$
b. $x \approx 3.3$
c. $x \approx -.8$

4. a. 2.3
b. -2.6
c. 49°

5. a. 8
b. approximately 8

Computer Master 23

1. a. $\sin 72° = .951056505$
$\cos 72° = .30901703$
b. Answers will vary. Most computers calculate to a greater degree of accuracy than most calculators.

2. a. $\sin 30° = .499999986$
$\cos 30° = .866025911$
b. $\sin 30° = .5$
$\cos 30° = \dfrac{\sqrt{3}}{2}$
c. $\sin 45° = \cos 45° = .7071068$
d. $\sin 45° = \cos 45° = \dfrac{\sqrt{2}}{2}$
e. Many answers are possible. Computers can not print irrational numbers such as $\sqrt{3}$; they only print finite decimal approximations. Approximating in the conversion from degrees to radians also introduces a source of error

3. a. 25 FOR D = 0 TO 90
            STEP 5
     45   NEXT D
     delete line 10
b. 80°, 35°, 75°
c. The Complements Theorem

4. a. 25 FOR D = 0 TO 360
            STEP 10
b. maximum $= 1$; minimum $= -1$
c. maximum $= 1$; minimum $= -1$
d. $\sin(D)$ is positive; $\cos(D)$ is negative
e. $90° < D < 270°$
f. $180° < D < 270°$
g. Many answers are possible. Sample: $\sin(D) > 0$ for $0° < D < 180°$; $\sin(D) = 0$ when $D = 0°$, $180°$ or $360°$; $\sin(D) < 0$ for $180° < D < 360°$. $\cos(D) > 0$ for $0° < D < 90°$ or $270° < D < 360°$; $\cos(D) = 0$ when $D = 90°$ or $270°$; $\cos(D) < 0$ for $90° < D < 270°$.

5. a. True
b. Samples: $\sin(D + 90°) = \cos(D)$, $\sin(90° - D)$
$\cos(D + 90°) = -\sin(D)$, $-\cos(90° - D)$
c. Many answers are possible. Samples: $\cos(D + 180°) = -\cos(D)$, $\sin(360° + D) = -\sin(D)$

6. b. $\sin(2D)$
c. the second formula

Computer Master Answers
Advanced Algebra © Scott, Foresman and Co.

Computer Master 24

1. a. $-360, -180, 0, 180, 360, 540$
 b. 1
 c. -1
 d. $-1 \le y \le 1$
 e. $-270, 90, 450$
 f. 810
 g. $90 + 360n$

2. a. $-270, -90, 90, 270, 450$
 b. $-1 \le y \le 1$
 c. $(-315, .7)(-135, -.7)$
  $(45, .7)(225, -.7)(405, .7)$
 d. $45 + 180n$

3. a. $.6; 36$
 b. $54; -54$
 c. $-.9; -117$
 d. $25; 155$

4.

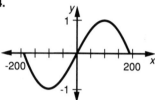

5. sine; $n = 360$ or any multiple of 360

6. a. $-180, 0, 180$
 b. no
 c. $0.3, -3.7, -1.0$
 d. 11.4; no, the function has no maximum value

7. a. changes amplitude; maximum value of f is $|k|$, and minimum is $-|k|$
 b. changes period; period is $\dfrac{2\pi}{|k|}$
 c. shifts vertically k units

Computer Master 25

1. a. 3.14159266
 b. .7
 c. 120°
 d. 60°

2. a. 1.064628; 1.169346; 1.291516
 b. 57°, 57.3°

3. a.

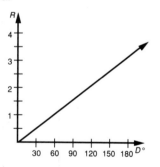

 b. Yes; $\dfrac{\pi}{180}$; 0

4. a. .9
 b. 5; $-450°, -270°, -90°, 90°, 270°$
 c. 3; $-360°, 0°, 360°$
 d. 2; 78°, 282°

5. b. Use -3.14 to 3.14

6. a. 1.0
 b. .6
 c. .8, 2.4
 d. $-1.6, 4.7$
 e. 4; 1.0, 2.2, $-4.1, -5.7$

Computer Master 26

1. a. 3
 b. 3
 c. $(8, 0)(-2, 0)\left(\dfrac{3}{5}, 0\right)$
 d. $8, -2,$ and $\dfrac{3}{5}$

2. a. $1, 4, -\dfrac{7}{2}$
 b. $1, 4, -\dfrac{7}{2}$
 c. Sample: The second is a reflection image of the first over the x-axis.

3. a. $f(x) = (x + 6)(x - 3)(x - 5)$
 b. Samples:
  $f(x) = (x + 6)(3 - x)(x - 5)$ or
  $f(x) = (x + 6)(x - 3)(5 - x)$

4. a. $y = (x + 2)(2x - 3)(4x - 17)$
 b. $y = (x + 2)(x + 2)(2x - 3)$
  $(4x - 17)$
 c. $y = (x + 2)(x + 2)(2x - 3)$
  $(2x - 3)(4x - 17)$

5. b. $-6, -1, 4$
 c. $(x + 6)(x + 1)(x - 4)$

6. b. $2, -6, 3.5$
 c. $(x - 2)(x + 6)(2x - 7)$

7. a. $1, -3.5, 3, -.5$
 b. $(x - 1)(2x + 7)(x - 3)(2x + 1)$

8. b. 3
 c. Similar to $f(x) = (x - 3)^3$ but steeper
 e. For even n, the shape is like a U with vertex at $(a, 0)$ and points in Quadrants I and II. For odd n, the shape varies from a line for $n = 1$, to a curve for $n \ne 1$; all such curves go through $(a, 0)$ with $f(x)$ a large positive number when x is large, and $f(x)$ a small negative number when x is very small.

Computer Master 27

1. a. 3
 b. 1
 c. 1 and 2; -3 and 4; 0 and -1

2. a. 1.8
 b. 1.78
 c. $-3.3; -0.5$

3. a. 40   DEF FN F(X) = 2 * X ∧ 3
  + 15 * X ∧ 2 + 32 * X
  + 16
 b. Yes; -4
 c. $-3; -2.8; -2.78$
 d. -0.72

4. $-9.9, -1.3, 0.9, 2$

5. a. $2000x^8 + 2000x^7 + 2000x^6 + 2000x^5 + 2000x^4 + 2000x^3 + 2000x^2 + 2000x + 2000$
 b. $22982.6
 c. 10%

Computer Master 28

1. a. ellipse
 b. hyperbola
 c. parabola
 d. ellipse
 e. parabola

2. a. parabola; 16; 16
 b. ellipse; 64; 80
 c. hyperbola; 81; 0
 d. hyperbola; 49; -40
 e. parabola; 0; 0
 f. ellipse; 0; 24

3. $B^2 = 4AC$: parabola;
  $B^2 > 4AC$: hyperbola;
  $B^2 < 4AC$: ellipse

4. a. $C = 2$; parabola;
  $C > 2$; ellipse;
  $C < 2$; hyperbola
 b. $C = -6.75$: parabola;
  $C < -6.75$: ellipse;
  $C > -6.75$: hyperbola

5. $k = 9$

6. Only an hyperbola can be drawn. B can be any real value since $4AC = -96$ and $B^2 > -96$ for all real values of B.

7. $B^2 = (-7)^2 = 49$
  $4AC = 4(-8)(6) = -192$
  The graph is two lines, which is a degenerate hyperbola.

Computer Master 29

1. a. $2.93
   b. 2.39 million bushels
   c. about $7 million

2. a. $2.47
   b. about $7 million; The expected revenues are the same.
   c. At any point, price times quantity is the same.
   d. $2.80 × 2.21 = 6.188; $2.41 × 2.73 = 6.579; The products are not equal so the elasticity is not 1.

3. a. (23, 31) and (10, −60)
   b. region A
   c. They would be the same. The points of intersection might be different, but would always lie on the same line.
   d. Multiply each temperature by the fraction of the total area for the region and then add those products.

4. a. (23, 31), (87, 39), (10, −60), (−4, 52)
   b. Yes, but it would then be necessary to locate the intersection of the lines.
   c.

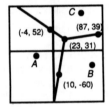

Computer Master 30

1. 5   107   285

2. 15   −147   −945

3. 224

4. 1176

5. 1470

6. 93

7. a. 208 feet
   b. 784 feet

8. 14 seconds

9. 6   1215   1820

10. 11   .0234375   47.9765625

11. a. 12   −4194304   −3355443

12. a. ≈794.1
   b. ≈928.2
   c. $n \geq 29$
   d. S_n can get as close to 1000 as we wish, because
   $$\lim_{n \to \infty} S_n = \frac{100}{1 - (.9)} = 1000.$$
   But S_n will never exactly equal 1000.

13. 1364 letters